Uplifting

PRAYERS

TO LIGHT YOUR WAY

ALSO BY SONIA CHOQUETTE

CD Programs

*Ask Your Guides: How to Connect with Your
Spiritual Support System* (6-CD and 4-CD sets)

*Attunement to Higher Vibrational Living,
with Mark Stanton Welch* (4-CD set)

*How to Trust Your Vibes at Work
and Let Them Work for You* (4-CD set)

*Meditations for Receiving Divine Guidance,
Support, and Healing* (2-CD set)

The Power of Your Spirit: A Guide to Joyful Living (6-CD set)

*Trust Your Vibes at Work,
and Let Them Work for You* (4-CD set)

Trust Your Vibes: Secret Tools for Six-Sensory Living (6-CD set)

Uplifting
PRAYERS
TO LIGHT YOUR WAY

200
Invocations
FOR
Challenging
Times

SONIA CHOQUETTE

HAY HOUSE, INC.
Carlsbad, California • New York City
London • Sydney • Johannesburg
Vancouver • Hong Kong • New Delhi

Published and distributed in the United States by: Hay House, Inc.:
www.hayhouse.com® • *Published and distributed in Australia by:*
Hay House Australia Pty. Ltd.: www.hayhouse.com.au • *Published
and distributed in the United Kingdom by:* Hay House UK, Ltd.:
www.hayhouse.co.uk • *Published and distributed in the Republic of
South Africa by:* Hay House SA (Pty), Ltd.: info@hayhouse.co.za • *Distributed in Canada by:* Raincoast Books: www.raincoast.com • *Published in India by:* Hay House Publishers India: www.hayhouse.co.in

Cover design: Amy Rose Grigoriou • *Interior design:* Riann Bender

ISBN: 978-1-4019-4453-7

Printed in the United States of America

I dedicate this book to my mother, Sonia Polixenia,
who taught me the power of prayer.

Contents

Cloudy Skies: *Prayers FOR A Troubled Mind* 59

Rainy Days: *Prayers FOR A Heavy Heart* 75

Thunderstorms and Lightning Strikes:
Prayers FOR Difficult Challenges 91

Lightening the Load: *Prayers TO Ease My Way* 141

New Horizons: *Prayers FOR More Love AND Light* 197

INTRODUCTION

I have prayed for as long as I can remember.

As a very young child, I prayed to my guardian angel, to Jesus, and to the all-loving and ever-present Holy Mother-Father God and asked for love and protection for myself and for my family. As a teenager, I added prayers to keep me grounded and safe . . . and to help me find a boyfriend. As a young woman just starting out in life, I included prayers for security, prayers for lessening my loneliness and fears, and prayers for financial support to help me pay my bills.

In my work, I began to pray for the health and well-being of my clients and students, and for the alleviation of their worries and concerns.

Once I got married and became a mother, I added prayers for my children, my husband, and my husband's family, as well as for help with all the problems and decisions we faced as a family. All my life I've also prayed for my friends and for people in need.

The reasons for prayer only grew as I grew. At the same time, the number of prayers answered also grew. As a result, I cannot imagine my life without prayer. It would be like trying to survive without oxygen. Prayer sustains my soul and comforts my anxious mind. And like oxygen, I can't live without it.

Prayer takes you out of your ego-based fears and returns you to your heart, where you feel love and support. It invites you to give up control and surrender all worries and concerns to a higher power. It gives you a break and takes the pressure off being human.

Most of all, prayer reminds us that we are never alone and can always count on receiving God's help if we ask for it. Prayer strengthens us with the confidence and courage we need to quiet our fears, follow our intuition, lead with our heart, and trust that all will be okay.

Praying has brought me so much relief, guidance, support, and comfort over the years that I've filled countless journals with my personal prayers. Every time I go back and reread those prayers, I am amazed by the ways in which they've all been answered.

Praying, for me, is an ongoing, very intimate conversation with my loving Creator. It is a time for me to share my fears, worries, pain, and hurt, and ask for God's assistance to get through whatever I am facing. It is a time to open my heart and place my faith in something greater than my limitations. It enables me to remain strong, clear, and loving no matter what is before me.

Prayer is also a time for celebration. I pray every day in gratitude for the experiences of that day. I say thanks for all the opportunities and blessings I've been given, and for all the help I wasn't even aware I was receiving.

Prayer When in Dire Need

Several years ago, I underwent a particularly challenging time, facing—only six weeks apart—the unexpected deaths of my brother and my father. And then, my marriage of 30 years imploded.

Bereft and filled with grief and anger, I got down on my knees and prayed for healing, as no other effort brought relief. What followed in answer to my prayers was the unexpected, intuitive guidance to walk—alone—the legendary Camino de Santiago, an 800-kilometer (500-mile) ancient pilgrimage over the Pyrenees and across Spain, which I did. I shared this experience in my book *Walking Home: A Pilgrimage from Humbled to Healed.*

With prayer as my constant companion and greatest source of strength, I was able to complete this arduous journey in mostly inclement weather, in spite of a recent knee surgery and with no experience (or preparation, for that matter) in long-distance hiking. With the power of prayer moving me forward, I eventually came to finish the pilgrimage and with it heal a lifetime of emotional pain and heartache, as well as discover a deep and lasting peace in my heart.

The power of prayer during that time is what inspired me to write this little prayer book.

More than any other moment in my entire life, I needed and asked for extra help in facing the challenges before me with endless prayers, both written down and spoken out loud, many times during the day if necessary . . . all of which kept me grounded, comforted, and able to move through the difficulties before me with grace. At times, my only prayers were *Help me, please,* and *Thank you. Thank you. Thank you in advance for answering my prayer.* Those were enough. My prayers were heard and answered, many beyond my wildest dreams.

I believe that you, too, can experience the same relief and inner guidance that I did through the amazing power of prayer.

———— ◆ ————

In the course of our lives, there come occasions when we're all asked to grow on a soul level. These transitions can be very challenging, even frightening. These are the moments when we face sudden and unexpected changes—loss, death, betrayal, sickness, and more—or enter into what is known as the "dark night of the soul." Life feels overwhelming and unsatisfying in a way we can no longer ignore, and we fall into despair, fearing that we have lost our way and may never find a happy and meaningful life again.

This prayer book is especially designed to be used during these periods of soul growth and challenge. Such times set us on a spiritual journey inward in which we are compelled to review our way of seeing and doing things. It is an opportunity to examine ourselves, our relationships, and our actions—in both our work and personal lives—to see if we are living up to our fullest and most authentic potential as souls. If not, we must find the courage to make the changes necessary to come back into holy alignment with our true selves. These are the times when we are called to take responsibility for our lives and do whatever we must to recommit to living as fully conscious, content, purposeful spiritual adults.

The soul journey inward is when we are invited to cast aside beliefs and behaviors that no longer serve us and release all tendencies toward victimhood, stagnation, passivity, and self-destruction that keep us disempowered or cause frustration and suffering to ourselves and others. This is no easy task, and one in which we can use all the divine support possible to help us on our way. It is a time to pray.

How This Book Is Organized

Like any other journey, the journey within unfolds in stages, each with its own set of challenges and unique opportunities to grow. I've structured this prayer book to support each stage of soul growth on this inward exploration so that you will find help every step of the way.

The first stage is called *Waking Up.* In this section, you will find prayers that ask for help in admitting unhappiness and finding the courage and strength to recognize where life is not working, is not satisfying, or does not reflect who you are and want to be. The prayers in this section ask for divine help to wake you up to your true path, especially when it seems overwhelming or impossible to do.

The next section, *Getting Ready,* offers prayers to help you prepare to make big life changes, such as facing your fears, embracing change, living a life of authenticity, and more . . . even if it means causing others disappointment or upsetting the status quo.

The next stage, *The Journey Begins,* offers prayers to help you shed the skin of your old life as you grow a new one. These prayers focus on such things as discovering your soul's true goals, believing in yourself, and connecting with your soul's plan for this life.

The next five sections offer prayers for protection and healing. *Protection along the Way* helps you create healthy personal boundaries, cut ties with what is not good for your spirit, and keep clear of negative energies as you travel back to your authentic self. *Cloudy Skies* addresses the mental troubles that rob you of your peace of mind, and *Rainy Days* focuses on the emotional ups and downs that keep you feeling unhappy. *Thunderstorms and Lightning Strikes* enables you to manage unsettling events and struggles that throw you off balance, and *Blue Skies* ensures that you learn the spiritual lessons that will restore you to inner peace and balance.

In *Following the Signs,* you will find prayers for following subtle, intuitive signs leading back to your spirit, as well as prayers to help with your changing relationships—both those you are leaving and those you hope to create. It also offers prayers for dealing with other people, especially difficult ones, along the way.

Lightening the Load offers prayers to help you let go of ego perceptions and patterns that make life painful and difficult. Following is *Fellow Travelers,* which focuses on prayers for managing difficulties with other human beings, as well as prayers for attracting positive, supportive relationships into your life.

Enjoying the Journey provides you with prayers that allow you to open up to new ways of being, doing, and experiencing yourself as a divine spirit and entering into a brand-new, far more congruent, uplifting, and authentic way of life. These prayers support your full alignment with your spirit and your soul's holy plan.

New Horizons offers prayers for finding compassion, kindness, and gratitude for recognizing and experiencing the beauty and love all around you. The final stage, *Coming Home to My Spirit,* focuses on gratitude, love, appreciation, and blessings. These prayers fill your life with inner peace and calm.

You will also notice that every prayer opens with the same beginning, calling in the Love and Light of the Holy Mother-Father God. The repetition of this opening invocation conditions your mind to become quiet and receptive to divine support the moment you say these words and draws you into a deeper state of receptivity so that you are better able to receive the love and blessings you are asking for. Moreover, each prayer ends with a thank-you and an acknowledgment that your prayer will be heard. This ending serves as an act of faith and allows you to surrender your prayer into God's hands.

How and When to Pray

It's easy to pray.

To pray successfully, the only thing you need is the ability to feel your prayer in your heart. Don't worry about lack of faith. Pray for faith if you feel doubtful, but just be sincere. That's all.

You may pray silently or aloud, as you prefer. I pray aloud as often as I can, as hearing the sound of my own voice in prayer quickly silences the other voices in my head and calms my spirit. Of course, it's not always convenient to pray out loud, so do know that praying silently is just as powerful. The important thing is not to worry too much about how to pray, and just pray. How you pray is *your* way and *right* for you.

How to Use This Book

There are many ways to use this book:

- You may want to start at the beginning and follow a prayer a day. Or you might want to open to the specific section that best reflects where you are in life, and then read and contemplate those prayers.

- You may want to open to a random page each morning as a way to start the day. Read the little prayer out loud if possible, and then sit quietly for a moment or two and feel the prayer in your heart. Breathe the prayer in, and send it to God as you breathe out. Once it's sent, let your heart rest, knowing that God will receive and answer it. Have faith, and let go of any worries or concerns.

- If not in the morning, perhaps you may want to open this book at midday and read a prayer, especially if your day is challenging.

- Another good time to pray is before meals. Read a prayer from the book to nourish your spirit just as you are about to nourish your body.

- Of course, right before sleep is also a
  perfect time to open this prayer book.
  Ending the day with a prayer allows you
  to turn all your concerns and needs over
  to God and his divine helpers, angels, and
  guides to work on while you sleep.

In other words, it's *always* a good time to pray, so
use this book whenever you feel compelled to do so,
day or night. Here are a few more helpful uses:

- Use a bright marker to circle your favorite
  prayers, or place colored tabs on the pages
  with prayers that resonate with you the
  most. That way you can return to those
  prayers again and again, saying them
  out loud, releasing them to God, and
  strengthening your faith as you do.

- You may also want to first read a prayer
  and then write one of your own below
  or next to it. Let these prayers serve as a
  springboard to your heart, where you'll
  find your prayers waiting to be expressed
  and sent to God.

- Finally, if you aren't averse to the idea, cut
  out the prayers in this book that speak to

you, and post them in places you'll see them again and again. Prayers work if you use them, and this is a great way to do so. I have little prayers posted all over my home. Whenever I stop before one, I say it out loud. This warms my heart, comforts my sprit, and connects me to God over my fears.

Be creative in how you use this book; make it yours. Carry it with you. Mark it up. Use it! There are even a few blank pages at the end for you to write your own prayers. Let this book bring you peace and comfort and calm your soul. Above all, allow this book to help you open a personal dialogue with the Holy Mother-Father God, Divine Loving Light and Heart of the Universe, who loves you always.

I hope in these pages you find solace, reassurance, renewed faith, and a deeper connection to God's endless love for you as you journey back to your authentic self. You are a beautiful light in the Universe, and hopefully these prayers will guide you to that realization.

It is my prayer, above all, that this book brings you peace in difficult times and helps you celebrate the joyous times. If you use it, I am confident that it will.

All my love,
Sonia

Waking Up

Prayers
TO
Reconnect
WITH
Your Spirit

———— ❧ ————

    In this section, you will find prayers that ask for help recognizing unhappiness and finding the courage to admit where life is not working, is not satisfying, or does not reflect who you are and who you want to be. The prayers in this section request divine help to wake up your sleeping spirit, move back into integrity with your true self, and find the inner strength to make the changes necessary to come back into alignment with your spirit. You will feel guided as you take the first steps on the journey back to self.

Waking My Spirit Up

Holy Mother-Father God,
Divine Loving Light and Heart of the Universe,

I humbly ask for the healing power of your grace to stir the fire in my belly and wake up my sleeping spirit. Shake me out of the complacency I've been in, and get me excited about my life once again. Please open my eyes so that I may see what I have missed, my ears so that I may hear what I have ignored, and my awareness so that I may appreciate the beauty I have failed to witness and use it to create something beautiful in my life now. I have become disconnected from my spirit and lost touch with my inner light. Send in your angels to dance through my being and give me the grace to fully explore life with a childlike sense of discovery. I thank you in advance, with my whole heart and soul, for answering my prayer, and I confidently await these blessings.

Amen and with infinite gratitude.

Being True to Myself

Holy Mother-Father God,
Divine Loving Light and Heart of the Universe,

I humbly ask for the healing power of your grace to find me, as I have abandoned myself. Breathe your most holy breath into my being and cleanse my soul of all that is not in support of my true nature. I pray for you to free me of all attachments that do not serve me and lead me to those that do. Let me be honest about my own motivations when dealing with others, and keep me from indulging in unworthy manipulations and self-serving, ego-based maneuvers at the expense of my authenticity and spirit. Please send in your angels to move me back into the flow of an authentic life. I thank you in advance, with my whole heart and soul, for answering my prayer, and I confidently await these blessings.

Amen and with infinite gratitude.

Shaking Things Up

Holy Mother-Father God,
Divine Loving Light and Heart of the Universe,

I humbly ask for your healing grace to allow me to have new experiences. Please send in your angels to keep me from sticking to the same routines, as I fear I will become stuck forever. Wake me out of this trance and help me get my mojo back by guiding me to do something brand-new and totally out of my comfort zone. I thank you in advance, with my whole heart and soul, for answering my prayer, and I confidently await these blessings.

Amen and with infinite gratitude.

———— ◆ ————

Growing Up

Holy Mother-Father God,
Divine Loving Light and Heart of the Universe,

I humbly ask for the healing power of your grace to help me grow into the beautiful Light that I am. Please help me leave behind childish fears and expectations, the need for approval of authority, and the belief that others should take care of me. Please send in your angels to help me live without fear, expect good things as the result of my own efforts, approve of myself, and be responsible for and committed to my happiness and security. I thank you in advance, with my whole heart and soul, for answering my prayer as I confidently step into my power.

Amen and with infinite gratitude.

Committing to What I Love

Holy Mother-Father God,
Divine Loving Light and Heart of the Universe,

I humbly ask for the healing power of your grace to help me fully commit to what I love and what calls to my heart. Please send in your angels to help me do all that I can this day to further the life I really want and quit waiting for it to come to me. Help me put two feet in and fully surrender myself to the things and people that are important to me, instead of avoiding commitment for fear of failure. I pray, give me the courage and grace to make it my priority to put forth my full attention, heart, and effort to all that calls me, and push me to take the leap of faith necessary to fearlessly go after my goals. I thank you in advance, with my whole heart and soul, for answering my prayer, and I confidently await these blessings this day.

Amen and with infinite gratitude.

——— ◆ ———

Finding the Courage to Be Who I Really Am

Holy Mother-Father God,
Divine Loving Light and Heart of the Universe,

I humbly ask for the healing power of your grace to help me find the courage to face all the consequences that come with being who I really am. Grant me the strength to free myself from what is not right for my spirit at this time, even if it frightens me to do so. Please send in your angels to help me follow my heart and ignore the protests of my ego or of others. Surround me with divine protectors who will remove any obstacles and obstructions, and will embolden me as I return to my true self. I thank you in advance, with my whole heart and soul, for answering my prayer and giving me the strength I need to do this.

Amen and with infinite gratitude.

———— ◆ ————

Being Real

Holy Mother-Father God,
Divine Loving Light and Heart of the Universe,

I humbly ask for the healing power of your grace to grant me the courage to be authentic and not phony in any way. Grant me the blessing to unmask myself and reveal my true heart to others. Please send in your angels to help me overcome my fear of rejection, and fill me with self-love so that I may allow others in. Release me from my tendency to buffer my heart with overly protective energy, causing me to feel isolated and alone. I thank you in advance, with my whole heart and soul, for answering my prayer and leading me back to love.

Amen and with infinite gratitude.

Welcoming Change

Holy Mother-Father God,
Divine Loving Light and Heart of the Universe,

I humbly ask for the healing power of your grace to help me meet the changes occurring in my life with confidence, knowing that all is unfolding for my highest good. I pray especially for the grace to have faith that those things that I did not expect are also for my highest good, even though I may not fully recognize this right now. I pray for your most holy blessing so that my inner light may shine brightly through the fog of these unclear passages as your loving presence guides me. I thank you in advance, with my whole heart and soul, for hearing my prayer, and I confidently await these blessings.

Amen and with infinite gratitude.

———— ◆ ————

Increasing Integrity

Holy Mother-Father God,
Divine Loving Light and Heart of the Universe,

I humbly ask for the healing power of your grace to help me keep my word, follow through on my commitments, and know my limits so that others can trust and rely on me. I pray, help me express myself clearly, kindly, and with love, no matter how uncomfortable it may feel to do this. Grant me the strength to honor my feelings and respect myself, regardless of what others say or think. By the same token, keep me from relying on those who cannot do this for me and help me to not take it personally. Please send in your angels to prevent me from taking advantage of anyone or letting them take advantage of me. I thank you in advance, with my whole heart and soul, for answering my prayer, and I look forward to the relief it will bring to me.

Amen and with infinite gratitude.

———— ◆ ————

Finding Purpose

Holy Mother-Father God,
Divine Loving Light and Heart of the Universe,

I humbly ask for your most blessed grace to fill me with a renewed sense of purpose, as I have been wasting my time on things that are not fulfilling to my spirit. This has left me feeling discouraged and dissatisfied. Please guide me back to what fulfills my soul and helps me utilize my unique gifts and skills in a way that serves my highest good and will make this a better world. Help me release all fear and confusion over how this will unfold, and let my intuition lead me to the right path. I pray for you to send in your angels to clear my way as I gracefully move toward my soul's true callings, even if only with baby steps. I thank you in advance, with my whole heart and soul, for answering my prayer, and I confidently await clear direction.

Amen and with infinite gratitude.

Facing Fears

Holy Mother-Father God,
Divine Loving Light and Heart of the Universe,

I humbly ask for the healing power of your grace to help me quit pretending that the life I have settled for is the one I want. Grant me the courage to be the person I long to be and make the changes I need in order to be happy. Please send in your angels to help me stop running from my fears and turn around and face them. Guide me to live a life of my dreams, even if I am afraid to step in that direction at the moment. I thank you in advance, with my whole heart and soul, for answering my prayer, and I confidently await these blessings.

Amen and with infinite gratitude.

Building a Directed Life

Holy Mother-Father God,
Divine Loving Light and Heart of the Universe,

I humbly ask for the healing power of your grace to return to me all the energy I have scattered so that I can use it to build a more loving, authentic life. Please send in your angels to help me stay the course of my new path so that I do not drift back to old ways of wasting time, procrastinating, and making excuses rather than showing up to the things that matter to my heart and spirit. I thank you in advance, with my whole heart and soul, for answering my prayer, and I confidently await these blessings this day.

Amen and with infinite gratitude.

———— ◆ ————

Being Responsible for My Happiness

Holy Mother-Father God,
Divine Loving Light and Heart of the Universe,

I humbly ask for the healing power of your grace to help me take full responsibility for my own happiness, rather than try to make others responsible for it. Please grant me the maturity and strength to begin making healthy, self-loving decisions and take the action I need to support my well-being in every way. Help me get excited about my life, do the things that I love, and take interest in what will challenge me in new ways. Help me leave the past behind and focus my attention on the moment and everything I can do now to support my spirit and contribute to my life and to others. I thank you in advance, with my whole heart and soul, for answering my prayer, and I look forward to living in the now.

Amen and with infinite gratitude.

—— ◆ ——

Getting Ready

Prayers

FOR

Beginning
Anew

※

In this section, you will find prayers that help you prepare to make the soul journey back to your authentic self by creating your heart's desire, setting priorities, embracing change, deciding to be the person you want to be today, and more. These prayers are designed to help you initiate positive changes in your life.

Returning to My True Path

Holy Mother-Father God,
Divine Loving Light and Heart of the Universe,

I humbly ask for the gift of your healing, as my life feels out of integrity with my spirit, and I can no longer tolerate this incongruent charade. Please grant me the courage to admit this deceit and faithfully begin the journey back to my true self. Please send in your angels to guide me through this passage with a loving and gentle heart, and keep me from harming others in the process. I thank you in advance, with my whole heart and soul, for answering my prayer, and I confidently await these blessings.

Amen and with infinite gratitude.

My Heart's Desire

Holy Mother-Father God,
Divine Loving Light and Heart of the Universe,

I humbly ask for the healing power of your grace to remove my uncertainty as I move toward new goals. Grant me the confidence to create my heart's desire and be free of excuses that prevent me from going after it. Please help me be consistent and not give up when things become difficult. Please send in your angels to assist me when I am challenged. I thank you in advance, with my whole heart and soul, for answering my prayer, and I confidently await these blessings.

Amen and with infinite gratitude.

Setting My Priorities

Holy Mother-Father God,
Divine Loving Light and Heart of the Universe,

I humbly ask for the healing power of your grace to turn my attention toward what is truly important and worthwhile, while ignoring all that is not. Please send in your angels to help me recognize the difference. I often get so confused that it's hard to determine where I should set my sights and focus my priorities. I thank you in advance, with my whole heart and soul, for answering my prayer, and I confidently await these blessings.

Amen and with infinite gratitude.

Quiet Action

Holy Mother-Father God,
Divine Loving Light and Heart of the Universe,

I humbly ask for your grace to help me stop talking about what I want to do, and just begin doing it instead. Enable me to stop living a virtual reality, full of dreams and ambitions that I take no actual steps to realize. Please send in your angels to help me cease wasting words so that I can channel this energy into action. I am ready to take real steps forward and ask your most holy assistance to support my dreams.

Amen and with infinite gratitude.

———— ◆ ————

Clearing Karma

Holy Mother-Father God,
Divine Loving Light and Heart of the Universe,

I humbly ask for the healing power of your grace to relieve the heaviness in my heart. If I have unfinished business, or karmic lessons I have yet to learn, please bring them to mind so that I might complete them now. If it is no more than a memory of pain, frozen in time, and serves no useful purpose today, please remove this sadness and replace it with lightness of being and peace in my heart. I thank you in advance, with my whole heart and soul, for answering my prayer, and I confidently await these blessings.

Amen and with infinite gratitude.

———— ◆ ————

Fear of Failure

Holy Mother-Father God,
Divine Loving Light and Heart of the Universe,

I humbly ask for the healing power of your grace to help me begin the things that I have been avoiding for fear of failure. Grant me the grace to move forward with confidence into the unknown. Please send in your angels to walk with me, especially in the moments when I cannot see my way. I thank you in advance, with my whole heart and soul, for answering my prayer, and I am grateful to have you by my side.

Amen and with infinite gratitude.

Embracing Change

Holy Mother-Father God,
Divine Loving Light and Heart of the Universe,

I humbly ask for the healing power of your grace to help me embrace the changes upon me (in my job, in my relationship, in my home) with dignity and faith. Allow me to trust that on the other side of this huge transition I will be safe, grounded, and further along in my soul's growth than I am now. Relieve my fear that these changes will take my security away from me. Let me place my security in your guidance and take it one day at a time. Let me release and let go, as I now must, and know that even though the process of change is difficult, the outcome will bring about wonderful new beginnings and opportunities that I am not aware of in the moment. Please send in your angels to help me accept what is and let go of my resistance to life as it unfolds. I thank you in advance, with my whole heart and soul, for answering my prayer, and I confidently await these blessings this day.

Amen and with infinite gratitude.

———— ◆ ————

Remembering to Breathe

Holy Mother-Father God,
Divine Loving Light and Heart of the Universe,

I humbly ask for the healing power of your grace to help me breathe instead of holding my breath. Allow me to release the fear that takes my breath away and replace it with faith in your protection and guidance as I work through this most challenging passage. Give me the confidence I need in order to breathe deeply and be fully present and available to life at this moment rather than braced against it, for fear of being harmed, rejected, or out of control. I thank you in advance, with my whole heart and soul, for answering my prayer, and I confidently await my inner room to breathe.

Amen and with infinite gratitude.

Getting On with It

Holy Mother-Father God,
Divine Loving Light and Heart of the Universe,

I humbly ask for your grace to help me seek new opportunities, rather than remain unsatisfied and do nothing. Wake up my confidence in knowing that this is a beautiful world full of possibility just waiting for me the moment I step in. Please send in your angels to direct my attention to the open doors ahead, and give me a gentle push in that direction. I thank you in advance, with my whole heart and soul, for answering my prayer.

P.S. I won't mind if it's a shove and not a push!

Amen and with infinite gratitude.

———— ✦ ————

Being the Person I Want to Be

Holy Mother-Father God,
Divine Loving Light and Heart of the Universe,

I humbly ask for the healing power of your grace to help me treat others with respect, no matter how they treat me. Please send in your angels to keep me from behaving in a way that does not reflect who I am and who I choose to be. Even if I am provoked, help me respond in a loving, kind, self-respecting, and grounded manner. I thank you in advance, with my whole heart and soul, for helping me face the people in my life who aggravate or upset me with decency and love.

Amen and with infinite gratitude.

Sticking to My Goals

Holy Mother-Father God,
Divine Loving Light and Heart of the Universe,

I humbly ask for the healing power of your grace to grant me the self-discipline to work on my goals every day and not scatter about empty words in place of action. Grant me your benevolent blessing to cease my excuses, remove my distractions, and overcome my fear of failure. I pray, please send in your beautiful angels to help me make one decision a day in service to my goals and follow through with action and a clear sense of purpose. I humbly ask for your holy presence to keep me focused on what I love over what I fear, and keep me moving toward my goals, one small step at a time. I thank you in advance, with my whole heart and soul, for answering my prayer, and I confidently await these blessings.

Amen and with infinite gratitude.

Get Moving

Holy Mother-Father God,
Divine Loving Light and Heart of the Universe,

I humbly ask for the healing power of your grace to help me dance or run or walk or Hula-Hoop . . . anything physical that will get me off my chair, away from my computer, out of my head, and into my body. Please send in your angels to keep me from making excuses and staying stuck in one place, and get me back into the beautiful rhythm of life. I thank you in advance, with my whole heart and soul, for answering my prayer, and I confidently await these blessings.

Amen and with infinite gratitude.

Going Inward

Holy Mother-Father God,
Divine Loving Light and Heart of the Universe,

Grant me the wisdom to know when it is time to break away from others and be alone with my thoughts and my spirit. Help me protect my inner peace by avoiding excessive indulgence in those things that bring me down and demoralize me, such as watching the news or surfing the Internet. Please send in your angels to help me step inward and seek renewal each day in prayer and meditation. I thank you in advance, with my whole heart and soul, for helping me protect my serenity.

Amen and with infinite gratitude.

Karma and Lessons

Holy Mother-Father God,
Divine Loving Light and Heart of the Universe,

If I have karma to fulfill, help me do so quickly, consciously, and with a loving heart. If I have lessons to learn, bring them on and fill me with the grace to learn them without complaint. If I have forgiveness to offer, wake me out of the power trip that denies such a blessing and free me from my own chains of ignorance. Please send in your angels to help me grow in every way. I am ready. I thank you in advance, with my whole heart and soul, for answering my prayer, and I confidently await these blessings.

Amen and with infinite gratitude.

The Journey Begins

Prayers
FOR
Positive Change

—✕— ❖ —✕—

In this section, you will find prayers to help you embark upon the journey inward. These prayers focus on believing in yourself, showing up with love to your new commitments, adapting to change, finding self-discipline, discovering your goals, and more. Using these prayers will help you take significant steps that lead in the direction of your heart and true spirit.

Discovering My Goals

Holy Mother-Father God,
Divine Loving Light and Heart of the Universe,

I humbly ask for the healing power of your grace to help me discover what my spirit wants and believe that I absolutely deserve to have it. Help me explore the things that I am now drawn to without guilt or hesitation, and give myself a chance to develop these interests without the need to be good at them. Allow me to have a beginner's heart and mind so that I can rediscover the world with childlike curiosity and freedom all over again. I thank you in advance, with my whole heart and soul, for helping me live my life to the fullest.

Amen and with infinite gratitude.

Fight-or-Flight Reactions

Holy Mother-Father God,
Divine Loving Light and Heart of the Universe,

I humbly ask for the healing power of your grace to help me stay grounded and calm, even when I feel threatened. Please send in your angels to enable me to take ten breaths before I speak or act when I am triggered into a fight-or-flight response, causing me to say or do something that I might later regret. Please let my higher self take over when I do finally respond. I thank you in advance, with my whole heart and soul, for answering my prayer, as I know this will bring me greater peace.

Amen and with infinite gratitude.

Accomplishing My Dreams Now

Holy Mother-Father God,
Divine Loving Light and Heart of the Universe,

I humbly ask for your blessing and grace to help me organize my life around my true goals, instead of trying to squeeze them into my overbooked life. Please help me commit to doing something I love every day with the same reliability with which I do what I must. Please send in the angels to help me create my heart's desire now instead of deferring my dreams to meet my obligations. I thank you in advance, with my whole heart and soul, for answering my prayer, and I look forward to a more balanced life.

Amen and with infinite gratitude.

———◆———

Believing in Myself

Holy Mother-Father God,
Divine Loving Light and Heart of the Universe,

I humbly ask for the healing power of your grace to help me believe in myself. Grant me the grace to believe in my worth and no longer question my value in the eyes of others. Bless me to show up this day as my best self and give my all to everything I do. Open my heart and keep me from withholding my energy, my enthusiasm, my effort, my commitment, and my love from anyone. Please send in your angels to help me fully engage in life. I thank you in advance, with my whole heart and soul, for answering my prayer, and I confidently await these blessings this day.

Amen and with infinite gratitude.

———— ◆ ————

Showing Up
with Love

Holy Mother-Father God,
Divine Loving Light and Heart of the Universe,

I humbly ask for the healing power of your grace to help me show up with love to my work and do my very best. Please send in your angels so that I may serve my obligations as if I were serving you. Give me the strength and focus to treat everyone at work, co-workers and clients alike, as if they were the most important people in the world—as an act of the love I wish to express. I thank you in advance, with my whole heart and soul, for bringing me the joy I know will come from this decision.

Amen and with infinite gratitude.

Adapting to New Things

Holy Mother-Father God,
Divine Loving Light and Heart of the Universe,

I humbly ask for the healing power of your grace to help me become more flexible. Help me ease my rigid ideas and resistant way of doing things and welcome in the new as a way of learning and growing and making life easier. Please send in your angels to help me be more resilient, open-minded, and curious so I can have fun with new things instead of fear them. I thank you in advance, with my whole heart and soul, for helping me regain my joy.

Amen and with infinite gratitude.

———— ◆ ————

My Soul Plan

Holy Mother-Father God,
Divine Loving Light and Heart of the Universe,

I humbly ask for the blessing of your grace to awaken me to my soul plan, using the gifts and talents you have given me to fulfill this purpose. Keep me from confusing my purpose with my profession, and please guide me to ways in which I can be of service in the world and find fulfillment in doing so. Help me do this, without attaching financial needs to this end. If it is your holy plan that my purpose and my day-to-day work are the same, I trust you will lead me there. For now, please send in your angels to keep my confusion and need for control out of the way and lead my spirit to serve where I can be most useful. I thank you in advance, with my whole heart and soul, for answering my prayer, as I know this new direction will fulfill my heart.

Amen and with infinite gratitude.

My Inner Peace

Holy Mother-Father God,
Divine Loving Light and Heart of the Universe,

I humbly ask for the ability to stay focused on what is important for my inner peace and well-being right now and ignore all else. Grant me the strength and courage to immediately remove myself from negative influences or people that disturb my spirit or encourage me to disrespect myself or others, and help redirect my energy toward that which is supportive, uplifting, and healthy. Please send in your angels to help me slow down long enough to assess my situation and make choices that protect my peace as I move through the day. I thank you with my whole heart and soul for bringing me to the realization that I need to make these kinds of self-loving decisions in my life right now. I ask for the discipline and self-love to honor these intentions.

Amen and with infinite gratitude.

Freedom from Selfishness

Holy Mother-Father God,
Divine Loving Light and Heart of the Universe,

I humbly ask for the healing power of your grace to help me recognize when I may be acting in selfish or unloving ways. Please send in your angels to help me stop justifying my righteous behaviors, quickly admit my mistakes, and apologize to the people I have hurt. I thank you in advance, with my whole heart and soul, for helping me bring more love and healing to myself and others in this way.

Amen and with infinite gratitude.

———— ◆ ————

Self–Discipline

Holy Mother-Father God,
Divine Loving Light and Heart of the Universe,

I humbly ask for the healing power of your grace to help me stop making excuses so that I can begin the work necessary to achieve what I desire in life, rather than wait for others to bring it to me. Encourage me to "suit up, shut up, and show up" to what I want and dedicate myself fully to what matters most to my heart, starting today. I especially ask that you send in your angels to keep me from demanding from others what I don't ask of myself. Help me to act like an adult and take consistent steps toward creating rather than complaining. I thank you in advance, with my whole heart and soul, for answering my prayer, as I am tired of doing things the old way.

Amen and with infinite gratitude.

———— ◆ ————

Protection along the Way

Prayers

FOR

Healthy Boundaries

In this section, you will find prayers for energetic protection and extra support as you begin to make real changes in your life. These prayers focus on finding freedom from negative influences; learning to observe, not absorb, others' energy; stepping back and saying no; helping you stop overgiving and overdoing; and more. Using these prayers will allow you to remain grounded and keep you from being pushed around by energies that do not uplift and support you.

Pursuing and Protecting My Dreams

Holy Mother-Father God,
Divine Loving Light and Heart of the Universe,

I humbly ask for the healing power of your grace to protect my dreams by not allowing me to share them with those who cannot hear me or with those who will not be supportive of my decision to go after them. I ask for your blessing as I turn to meditation instead and share my plans with you. Enable me to protect my heart as though it were a beautiful garden, inviting in those who will enjoy it with me and keeping out those who want to trample on it. Thank you for helping me help myself.

Amen and with infinite gratitude.

Freedom from Others' Negative Influence

Holy Mother-Father God,
Divine Loving Light and Heart of the Universe,

I humbly ask for the healing power of your grace to clear my mind, as it is flooded with the opinions of those around me, and I have lost the connection with my spirit. Grant me the blessing to silence others' voices in my head, especially the fearful ones, so that I may hear my own inner voice and find my way back to my true path. Please send in your angels to help me break free of those who tell me to distrust what I feel, and keep me from soliciting their opinions. Let me honor my spirit fully instead. I thank you in advance, with my whole heart and soul, for clearing the mental static I have and bringing me back to peace.

Amen and with infinite gratitude.

Cutting Cords

Holy Mother-Father God,
Divine Loving Light and Heart of the Universe,

I humbly ask for the healing power of your grace to help me cut the invisible cords that bind me to the past so that I am able to fully and freely step into the present and be who I authentically am today. Grant me the inner wisdom to see and follow the highest path for me now as I move into my power. Please ask your angels to guide me to the best people and opportunities for me today, and grant me the wisdom to reach out and connect with them. I thank you in advance, with my whole heart and soul, for giving me the strength to move ahead and leave the past behind.

Amen and with infinite gratitude.

Stepping Back

Holy Mother-Father God,
Divine Loving Light and Heart of the Universe,

I humbly ask for the healing power of your grace to help me know when to step in and help others, and when to step back and not interfere. Please enable me to energetically stay in my own skin instead of inserting myself into what is not my concern. Grant me the wisdom to treat others as adults and not try to take over their responsibilities. Allow me to trust others to handle things for themselves. Please send in your angels to remind me to wait for others to ask for help before imposing it on them. I thank you in advance, with my whole heart and soul, for answering my prayer, and I confidently await these blessings.

Amen and with infinite gratitude.

Observing,
Not Absorbing, Energy

Holy Mother-Father God,
Divine Loving Light and Heart of the Universe,

I humbly ask for the healing power of your grace to keep me from absorbing other people's energy or becoming overwhelmed by their needs, and in the process surrendering my own boundaries. Strengthen my ability to listen to others while remaining calm and lovingly detached. Please send in your angels to keep me from being swept into taking care of others as a means of managing the stress they create in me. I pray for the power to offer others love and support without losing myself. I thank you in advance, with my whole heart and soul, for answering my prayer and helping me learn to take better care of myself.

Amen and with infinite gratitude.

Freedom from Unhappy and Broken Relationships

Holy Mother-Father God,
Divine Loving Light and Heart of the Universe,

I humbly ask for the healing power of your grace to burn away the deadwood of my sorrow and pain so that I may experience freedom from my unhappy and broken relationships and move on. Grant me the grace to send everyone from my past unconditional love and blessings. May the suffering and pain we have caused each other go away. I thank you in advance, with my whole heart and soul, for answering my prayer, and I confidently await my emotional healing.

Amen and with infinite gratitude.

Distance from Those Who Don't Treat Me Well

Holy Mother-Father God,
Divine Loving Light and Heart of the Universe,

I humbly ask for the healing power of your grace to help me set high, self-respecting standards for how I want to be treated in life and accept nothing less from others. Grant me the good sense and self-love to peacefully walk away from those who do not respect me or treat me well. Please send in your angels to keep me from taking offense at their behavior; instead, let me choose to love and forgive them as I remove myself from their presence. I thank you in advance, with my whole heart and soul, for answering my prayer and helping me learn to love myself.

Amen and with infinite gratitude.

Saying No

Holy Mother-Father God,
Divine Loving Light and Heart of the Universe,

I humbly ask for the healing power of your grace to help me recognize my limits and say *no* without guilt before I explode—or implode—under pressure. Please send in the angels to enable me not to feel intimidated or bullied into doing what I do not want to do or giving more than I want to give. Grant me the courage to speak up and draw the line when others are pushing me too far, in a loving but firm manner. Let me do this so that everyone in my life is clear about my boundaries, and I can eliminate the stress that comes from my being taken advantage of. I thank you in advance, with my whole heart and soul, for answering my prayer, and I look forward to the freedom this will bring.

Amen and with infinite gratitude.

Vulnerability

Holy Mother-Father God,
Divine Loving Light and Heart of the Universe,

I humbly ask for the healing power of your grace to help me accept my vulnerabilities, rather than believe they are something I should hide or be ashamed of. Please send in your angels to encourage me to have unconditional love for myself, just as I am. I thank you in advance, with my whole heart and soul, for answering my prayer and enabling me to love all of myself.

Amen and with infinite gratitude.

Stop Overgiving and Overdoing

Holy Mother-Father God,
Divine Loving Light and Heart of the Universe,

I humbly ask for the healing power of your grace to help me stop overdoing for and overgiving to others, while remaining insensitive and unloving toward myself. Please send in your angels to keep me from trying to earn love through these draining behaviors and allow me to know that I am always loved, no matter what I do. I thank you in advance, with my whole heart and soul, for answering my prayer and helping me relax and let go.

Amen and with infinite gratitude.

Standing Up
for Myself

Holy Mother-Father God,
Divine Loving Light and Heart of the Universe,

I humbly ask for the ability and courage to speak up and set clear boundaries, and not allow myself to be intimidated or feel threatened by someone (my boss, partner, parent, sibling, and so forth), or made to feel as though I must submit to another's wants and desires while I disrespect or disregard my own needs. Ground me in self-love and clarity as I firmly resist falling prey to all coercions, maneuvers, guilt trips, and false emergencies so that I can meet my authentic responsibilities to others in a healthy, loving way. I thank you in advance, with my whole heart and soul, for giving me the self-love and self-respect I need in order to grow in this way.

Amen and with infinite gratitude.

———— ◆ ————

Protecting My Peace

Holy Mother-Father God,
Divine Loving Light and Heart of the Universe,

I humbly ask for the blessing of your grace to walk away from people and things that disturb my spirit, drain my energy, and leave me feeling empty. Please send in your angels to help me run from drama and not create any myself. Grant me the grace to protect my peace and use my energy to create something positive instead. I thank you in advance, with my whole heart and soul, for enabling me to choose peace for myself.

Amen and with infinite gratitude.

Minding My
Own Business

Holy Mother-Father God,
Divine Loving Light and Heart of the Universe,

I humbly ask for the healing power of your grace to help me respect others' boundaries and not interfere with their lives as a way to make myself feel useful or worthy of love. Please send in your angels so that I can discern what is my business and what is not, and keep me focused on improving myself instead of coaching others on how to improve. I thank you in advance, with my whole heart and soul, for answering my prayer, and I look forward to the freedom this will bring to us all.

Amen and with infinite gratitude.

Discernment

Holy Mother-Father God,
Divine Loving Light and Heart of the Universe,

I humbly ask for the healing power of your grace to meet everyone with a pure heart and a clear mind. Grace me with better discernment so that I have an accurate assessment of those with whom I engage. Please send in your angels to help me see other people's strengths, as well as accept their limitations, so that I have realistic expectations of them and quit setting myself up for disappointment and heartbreak. I thank you in advance, with my whole heart and soul, for answering my prayer and keeping me grounded in reality over fantasy.

Amen and with infinite gratitude.

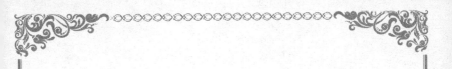

Cloudy Skies

Prayers

FOR A

*Troubled
Mind*

In this section, you will find prayers for relief from negative habits and energies that cloud your vision, weigh heavily on your mind, and cause distraction and distress to your spirit as you journey back to your authentic self. You will also find prayers that help with relieving anxiety, insecurity, and overcontrolling tendencies, as well as prayers for patience, freedom from drama, and more.

Anxiety

Holy Mother-Father God,
Loving Light and Heart of the Universe,

I humbly ask for your most blessed grace to calm my anxious heart. Please help remove my uneasiness and place my trust in the future into your loving care. Please send in the angels to reaffirm my faith that in spite of so many unexpected changes in my life at this time, all will work out. Please relieve me of the distress I now feel. Help me transmute this free-floating tension and worry into confident faith in myself and in my ability to address everything that comes my way in a competent, grounded manner. I am grateful for your constant love and support, and thank you, with my whole heart and soul, for answering my prayer.

Amen and with infinite gratitude.

Patience

Holy Mother-Father God,
Divine Loving Light and Heart of the Universe,

I humbly ask for the healing power of your grace to give me the gift of patience, which I am sorely lacking at the moment. Without it, I cause myself and others a lot of unnecessary stress and anxiety. Please help me relax and stop pushing for things to happen before their time. Allow me to step back, take a breath, and get into the flow, rather than trying to push the river of life to hurry up. Above all, remove the fear hiding underneath my impatience that I might miss out on something important if I am not the first in line to receive it. I thank you in advance, with my whole heart and soul, for answering my prayer, and I confidently await this desperately needed blessing.

Amen and with infinite gratitude.

———— ◆ ————

Insecurities
about Money

Holy Mother-Father God,
Divine Loving Light and Heart of the Universe,

I humbly ask for your most blessed grace to release my fear over not having enough money to meet my needs in the future and fill me with gratitude for the abundance you have already given me to meet my needs today. Please send in the angels to strengthen my faith in the continued flow of abundance and grace in my life and to leave me with peace of mind. I especially pray for new ideas and insights to help me increase my income as needed, and I ask for the flexibility and confidence to follow through on these inspirations when they appear. I thank you in advance, with my whole heart and soul, for answering my prayer . . . and in the meantime, I will relax.

Amen and with infinite gratitude.

———— ✦ ————

Self-Control

Holy Mother-Father God,
Divine Loving Light and Heart of the Universe,

I humbly ask for the healing power of your grace to rein in my overly impulsive behavior and check in with my objectivity and intuition—as well as with others, when they are affected—before I act. Please send in your angels to help me remain fully mindful of all the consequences of my choices and actions before I make them and to choose wisely in the days ahead. Keep me from overdoing, overspending, overtalking, overcommitting, and any other impulsive action before I have a moment to reflect on whether it is in my highest good. I thank you in advance for helping me contain my energy and make wise and grounded decisions. Thank you for hearing my prayer and calming me down.

Amen and with infinite gratitude.

Lifting My Spirit

Holy Mother-Father God,
Divine Loving Light and Heart of the Universe,

I humbly ask for the healing power of your grace to fully open my heart so that I may relish this gift of life that you have breathed into my body. I pray, send in your angels to help peel away any resistance I have to fully receiving and embodying the grace and goodness available to me now. Strip away all fear I have of feeling joy, even in the midst of challenge and change. Keep me mindful that everything in life is temporary so that I allow myself to fully experience and enjoy life now, while I can. I thank you in advance, with my whole heart and soul, for answering my prayer and lifting my spirit.

Amen and with infinite gratitude.

Releasing Control

Holy Mother-Father God,
Divine Loving Light and Heart of the Universe,

I humbly ask for the healing power of your grace to keep me from trying to control others as a way of feeling safe. Please allow me to let others be, without my interference. Grant me the wisdom to mind my own business and respect others' right to live their lives as they see fit. I especially ask for your help in doing this with my family (or grown children, co-workers, friends, partner, and so on). I pray, please send in your angels to help me love and accept others as they are and not try to change them into what I believe they should be. I thank you in advance, with my whole heart and soul, for answering my prayer, and I know the people in my life will soon be thanking you as well.

Amen and with infinite gratitude.

———— ◆ ————

Freedom from Drama

Holy Mother-Father God,
Divine Loving Light and Heart of the Universe,

I humbly ask for the healing power of your grace to recognize the ways in which I create drama, hurt myself and others, and block myself from giving and receiving love. I pray for the self-awareness to slow down, tune in to what I need, take responsibility for making healthy choices, and communicate with others in a loving, nondefensive, mature, and direct way rather than being passive-aggressive, withholding, or unforgiving, or acting out in immature, angry ways. Please send in your angels to help me walk away from other people's drama as well. Guide me to make choices that will allow me to succeed in my goals and relationships instead of engaging in behaviors that are sure to cause harm. I thank you in advance, with my whole heart and soul, for answering my prayer, and I am fully open to receiving your help now.

Amen and with infinite gratitude.

My Self-Worth

Holy Mother-Father God,
Divine Loving Light and Heart of the Universe,

I humbly ask for the healing power of your grace to help me be a peaceful, more content person. Grant me freedom from comparing myself to others or feeling inadequate and unworthy of love. Please send in your angels so that I might recognize my beautiful spirit and believe that my light, my gifts, and my contributions are worthy and meaningful. I thank you in advance, with my whole heart and soul, for answering my prayer and blessing me with your grace.

Amen and with infinite gratitude.

My Self–Doubt

Holy Mother-Father God,
Divine Loving Light and Heart of the Universe,

I humbly ask for the healing power of your grace to cast out the shadows and insecurities that cause me to doubt my value to others. Please send in your angels to help me see and value myself as you value me. Help me relax into a feeling of self-worth instead of being defensive and insecure about myself. I thank you in advance, with my whole heart and soul, for answering my prayer and relieving me of these fears.

Amen and with infinite gratitude.

Being Less Self-Centered

Holy Mother-Father God,
Divine Loving Light and Heart of the Universe,

I humbly ask for the blessing of your grace to help me be the kind of friend to others that I yearn to have. Please send in your angels to allow me to reach out and take interest in those around me, rather than remain absorbed in my own concerns. Grant me the grace to overcome my narcissistic tendencies and instead focus my attention on being supportive and nurturing. Let me extend my time and generosity and focus on how I can help people over what they can do for me. I know with your guidance my life will become more enriched, and I will experience deeper and more meaningful connections with others than I have allowed up until now. I thank you in advance, with my whole heart and soul, for answering my prayer, and I am open to all ways in which the answers come.

Amen and with infinite gratitude.

Relief from Perfectionism

Holy Mother-Father God,
Divine Loving Light and Heart of the Universe,

I humbly ask for the healing power of your grace to help me stop being so demanding and critical of myself. Grant me the grace to stop being a rigid perfectionist and strive to do my best rather than to live without flaw. Enable me to lovingly accept my imperfections and stay focused on my beautiful qualities instead. Please send in your angels to fill my heart with compassion and love for myself, and guide me to find peace within myself, just the way I am. Help me see myself through your eyes and stop trying to be perfect. This is my deepest prayer today.

Amen and with infinite gratitude.

———— ◆ ————

Impatience

Holy Mother-Father God,
Divine Loving Light and Heart of the Universe,

Thank you so much for sending me the gift of patience, which I have already asked for. It hasn't arrived yet, but I trust that it is on its way. I really look forward to receiving it, as do the people in my life who insist I need it. I am sure they will be thanking you shortly as well. This is my prayer for today.

Amen and with infinite gratitude.

Facing My Own Shadows

Holy Mother-Father God,
Divine Loving Light and Heart of the Universe,

I humbly ask for the healing power of your grace to help me honestly look at my own shadows, rather than point out those of others. Allow me to refrain from gossip, disparaging or criticizing others, or blaming them for my own unhappiness and dissatisfaction. I especially ask for help to recognize the faults in myself that I deny and begin the soul work necessary to become a clear channel of love and light in my own life and in the world. Give me the strength of character to see my limitations, admit my wrongdoings, address my addictions, and take the steps to become an emotionally healthy and sober person. This is my prayer today.

Amen and with infinite gratitude.

———— ◆ ————

Freedom from Negative Patterns Around Self–Care

Holy Mother-Father God,
Divine Loving Light and Heart of the Universe,

I humbly ask for the blessing of your grace to help me overcome my negative patterns around taking care of myself and begin to treasure myself with unconditional love and devotion to my well-being in every way. Please send in your angels so that I can adopt more self-loving and healthy patterns that will nourish and support my body, uplift my spirit, give me more physical and emotional strength, and help me show up in the world with vitality and confidence in who I am. I thank you in advance, with my whole heart and soul, for answering my prayer. I am ready for these changes.

Amen and with infinite gratitude.

Rainy Days

Prayers

FOR A

*Heavy
Heart*

In this section, you will find prayers that offer relief from emotional challenges, obstacles, setbacks, and heaviness that often darken the journey inward. Included are prayers that ask for help with depression, feeling overwhelmed, suffering, fear of being alone, heartache, grief, and more. Use these prayers to uplift your spirit and find relief from emotional pain.

Depression

Holy Mother-Father God,
Divine Loving Light and Heart of the Universe,

I humbly ask for your most blessed grace to lift the dark cloud I am under right now and help me trust that things will improve soon, both in my heart and in my life. Please send in your angels to lift me out of my malaise and discontent, and replace it with gratitude for everything in my life today and the energy to create a brighter tomorrow. Help me seek out and receive guidance from all true sources of support and healing so that I may once again feel joy. Awaken my spirit to the full recognition of all the glorious things that surround me and the wonderful people in my life who love and appreciate me as I am. Enable me to release all beliefs and fears that cause me to remain demoralized. I pray, send in your angels to chase away my feelings of depression so that I might experience a renewed enthusiasm for life. I thank you in advance, with my whole heart and soul, for answering my prayer and healing my sadness.

Amen and with infinite gratitude.

When Weary

Holy Mother-Father God,
Divine Loving Light and Heart of the Universe,

I humbly ask for your endless guidance and love as I work through my soul lessons in this life. The learning curve has been steeper than usual lately, and I am feeling weary from all the stress, so please send in extra angels to help me learn what I must. I thank you in advance, with my whole heart and soul, for answering my prayer and giving me a break.

Amen and with infinite gratitude.

Forgiving My Mistakes

Holy Mother-Father God,
Divine Loving Light and Heart of the Universe,

I humbly ask for the healing power of your grace to help me forgive myself, as I know you forgive me, for the mistakes I have made in the past and to free me of the shame I carry over my behavior. Help me learn from my mistakes so that I won't make them again and can let the past go now. Please send in your angels to light my way as I begin anew and move on in peace. I thank you in advance, with my whole heart and soul, for answering my prayer and trusting in the goodness of me.

Amen and with infinite gratitude.

Overwhelm

Holy Mother-Father God,
Divine Loving Light and Heart of the Universe,

I humbly ask for the healing power of your grace to help me place into your care everything that leaves me feeling overwhelmed and out of control. Please keep me grounded and allow me to step away when the energy around me, or the circumstances before me, become too much to handle at one time. Move me to go for a short walk, or allow myself a few quiet moments in order to regroup, so that I can respond to life from a grounded and clear state of mind. Please send in your angels to help me find the confidence and ability to do my very best, no matter what comes, even if I doubt myself at the moment. Enable me to give myself room to breathe and remember to take things more in stride. I thank you in advance, with my whole heart and soul, for answering my prayer and helping me today.

Amen and with infinite gratitude.

Clearing
Childhood Wounds

Holy Mother-Father God,
Divine Loving Light and Heart of the Universe,

I humbly ask for the healing power of your grace to bless and appreciate the infuriating messengers who push my buttons and remind me of my need to further clear and heal the emotional wounds from my childhood. Please help me recognize my reactive patterns for what they truly are, forgive the past, and fill myself with more self-love today. Allow me to address the root of my present aggravation and love myself unconditionally so that I can be free of this reactivity and peacefully live in the present. I thank you in advance, with my whole heart and soul, for hearing my prayer and offering me the love and grace I need in order to heal fully.

Amen and with infinite gratitude.

———— ◆ ————

When I'm Down

Holy Mother-Father God,
Divine Loving Light and Heart of the Universe,

I like to believe that I am strong, yet my heart is fragile at the moment. I like to believe I am hearty, even though I can barely carry on right now. I like to believe I am filled with power, although I feel powerless today. Please send in your angels to help fill me up with your strength, energy, and power so that I know all will be well. I thank you in advance, with my whole heart and soul, for answering my prayer and giving me the strength I need to carry on.

Amen and with infinite gratitude.

Stilling the Waters

Holy Mother-Father God,
Divine Loving Light and Heart of the Universe,

I humbly ask for the healing power of your grace to calm my agitated emotions. Grant me the grace to navigate the waters of my own turbulent feelings without getting lost at sea. Please send in the angels to row my boat for me, as I am struggling in this emotional storm. I thank you in advance, with my whole heart and soul, for answering my prayer, and I confidently await to be smooth sailing once again.

Amen and with infinite gratitude.

Freedom from Suffering

Holy Mother-Father God,
Divine Loving Light and Heart of the Universe,

I humbly ask for the healing power of your grace to help me break free of the bondage that keeps me attached to my own negative story. Please dissolve the subconscious strings that keep me tied to my own suffering. Please send in your angels to replace each string with a beam of light and love, leading directly back to you. I thank you in advance, with my whole heart and soul, for answering my prayer, and I look forward to the new story I am now creating.

Amen and with infinite gratitude.

Accepting Disappointment

Holy Mother-Father God,
Divine Loving Light and Heart of the Universe,

I humbly ask for the healing power of your grace to soothe my disappointed spirit. Please send me a sign that you are with me, as I feel so alone. Please also send in your angels to escort me out of this trap of feeling that all is lost, and let me know there is hope for the future, even if it is not the future I had hoped for. Let me accept my disappointment with grace and not take it personally. Grant me the ability to accept what happens in life and the knowledge that all is for the higher good. Allow me the strength of spirit to release all attachment to my unrealized expectations and hopes, and to surrender them to your better plan. I thank you in advance, with my whole heart and soul, for answering my prayer and soothing my soul.

Amen and with infinite gratitude.

Feeling Alone and Hopeless

Holy Mother-Father God,
Divine Loving Light and Heart of the Universe,

I humbly ask for the healing power of your grace to open my heart so that I may feel your presence. Please send in your angels to reassure me that I am never alone or unloved, as I now feel I am, because you are with me always. Please give me the ability to open my heart and allow for new connections and friends to come in and be made. Keep me from shutting myself away from the world and feeling hopeless and sorry for myself. I thank you in advance, with my whole heart and soul, for answering my prayer, and I confidently await feeling connected once again.

Amen and with infinite gratitude.

Healing Grief

Holy Mother-Father God,
Divine Loving Light and Heart of the Universe,

I humbly ask for the healing power of your grace to soothe my broken heart as I face the losses before me. I pray, please help me manage the grief I am now feeling. Please send in your angels to lift this heavy fog of pain as I slowly find my way forward. I accept the depth of my loss and know that this, too, is a holy moment in my life. Grant me the strength to carry on. I thank you in advance, with my whole heart and soul, for answering my prayer, and I am grateful you are with me at this time.

Amen and with infinite gratitude.

My Own Self–Undoing

Holy Mother-Father God,
Divine Loving Light and Heart of the Universe,

I humbly ask for the healing power of your grace to remove the blinders from my eyes and help me see my own undoing. Grant me the grace to become more aware of where and how I tune others out, cause problems, and isolate myself. Please send in your angels to help me remove the excessive guard around my heart so that I may be able to freely give and receive the love I yearn for. I thank you in advance, with my whole heart and soul, for answering my prayer and opening my heart.

Amen and with infinite gratitude.

Being Alone

Holy Mother-Father God,
Divine Loving Light and Heart of the Universe,

I humbly ask for the blessing of your grace to help me face my fear of being alone. Grant me the blessing of enjoying my own company instead of clinging, out of fear, to those whom I do not enjoy at all. Please send in your angels to help me find the confidence and inner peace to be at ease with myself at all times. I thank you in advance, with my whole heart and soul, for answering my prayer and helping me find comfort in my own being.

Amen and with infinite gratitude.

———— ✦ ————

More Patience, Please

Holy Mother-Father God,
Divine Loving Light and Heart of the Universe,

Thank you for sending me the gift of patience. I humbly ask if you meant to send more to me because I only received a little, and it is definitely not enough. If you have the chance, would you mind please sending me the rest? I thank you in advance for your extreme generosity in this matter. So do my friends and family.

Amen and with infinite gratitude.

———— ◆ ————

Rejection

Holy Mother-Father God,
Divine Loving Light and Heart of the Universe,

I humbly ask for your blessing and grace to soothe the burning rejection I feel in my heart. Please send in your angels to help me release this painful experience and learn the soul lesson that comes from it so that I can heal and move on. I trust in my heart that this is for my highest good in the end, but I am not at the end yet, so I need help to get there. I thank you in advance, with my whole heart and soul, for answering my prayer and easing my pain.

Amen and with infinite gratitude.

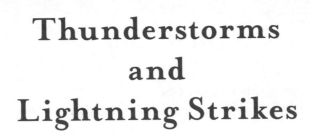

Thunderstorms and Lightning Strikes

Prayers

FOR

Difficult Challenges

————— ❦ —————

In this section, you will find prayers asking for support in meeting some of the challenging problems you might face on your journey back to your authentic self, such as help with addiction, resentments, or a chronically negative attitude. There are also prayers asking for relief from illness and help when feeling threatened, as well as protection from extreme stress, and more. Use them when you feel trapped or stuck, or if you fear that your problems are too big to handle alone.

Addiction

Holy Mother-Father God,
Divine Loving Light and Heart of the Universe,

I humbly ask for the healing power of your grace to remove my pride, vanity, denial, and resistance to admitting my addiction to (food, substances, and/or other addictions) and allow me to reach out and receive the help I need in order to overcome this devastation to my life. I pray, please send in your angels to enable me to readily acknowledge my powerlessness over the debilitating emotional wounds that cause this self-undoing and lead me to the light of love, healing, and support so I can return to a healthy, sober, peaceful life. I am so tired of my struggle and the shame and pain it brings upon me and others. I pray that you lift this burden from my life and help me heal. I thank you in advance, with my whole heart and soul, for answering my prayer.

Amen and with infinite gratitude.

Extreme Stress

Holy Mother-Father God,
Divine Loving Light and Heart of the Universe,

I humbly ask for the healing power of your grace to motivate me to make healthy, self-loving choices when it comes to how I treat myself. Please send in your angels with extra support to help me do this, especially when I am under extreme stress. Keep me from overdoing, overeating, overworking, or indulging in any substances. Rather than lashing out at those I love, allow me to meditate and relax instead. I thank you in advance, with my whole heart and soul, for answering my prayer and easing my stress.

Amen and with infinite gratitude.

Recovering from Illness

Holy Mother-Father God,
Divine Loving Light and Heart of the Universe,

I humbly ask for the healing power of your grace to help me fully recover from my illness today. Release me from all lack of self-love I may now consciously or unconsciously have, and fill my heart with forgiveness for all that has transpired in my life so that I may free up my own energy to bring about healing in my body as well. Grant me the resiliency that I need to overcome this hurdle and help me learn from this illness whatever hidden lesson it is trying to teach me so that I may return to full vitality. I thank you in advance, with my whole heart and soul, for answering my prayer, and I confidently await reclaiming my health once again.

Amen and with infinite gratitude.

———— ◆ ————

Chronically Negative Attitude

Holy Mother-Father God,
Divine Loving Light and Heart of the Universe,

I humbly ask for the healing power of your grace to help me let go of my negative attitude and change my perspective to a brighter one. Please send in your angels so that I may see the beauty and love all around me right now and be grateful for all the blessings I am given every day. Allow me to stop bracing myself against potential disappointment by having "worst-case scenario" expectations, thus diminishing my chance to feel real joy. Please help me lighten up and stop being a drag on the sails of my life. I thank you in advance, with my whole heart and soul, for answering my prayer and enabling me to see the goodness in life.

Amen and with infinite gratitude.

Surrendering Resentments

Holy Mother-Father God,
Divine Loving Light and Heart of the Universe,

I humbly ask for the healing power of your grace so that I may surrender all resentments I have toward [insert names of individuals] and find loving compassion for these and all the people in my life who have caused me pain. Please send in your angels to help transmute my negative energy into unconditional love for all so that I may be free to continue my life in peace. I thank you in advance, with my whole heart and soul, for answering my prayer and helping me open my heart and love freely once again.

Amen and with infinite gratitude.

Freedom from Anger

Holy Mother-Father God,
Divine Loving Light and Heart of the Universe,

I humbly ask for the healing power of your grace to liberate my mind and soul from the raging fires of anger besieging me right now. Please cool my anger and soothe this raw part of me with your comfort and love so that I may begin to heal and return to balance. I pray, send in your angels to help me take the actions of self-love necessary to purge these aggressive feelings I have toward some people and resurrect my sweet spirit from this inferno. I thank you in advance, with my whole heart and soul, for answering my prayer and bringing me back to peace.

Amen and with infinite gratitude.

Triggered

Holy Mother-Father God,
Divine Loving Light and Heart of the Universe,

I humbly ask for the healing power of your grace to help me stay calm and nonreactive around those who trigger my emotions. Please make me aware of what is going on inside of me that causes such a strong reaction to their behavior so I can free myself of this disturbance to my spirit. Please send in the angels to fill me with love for both of us, and show me what I need to heal in order to become neutral to the behavior of others. I humbly thank you, with my whole heart and soul, for keeping me calm in these moments.

Amen and with infinite gratitude.

Freedom from Fearmongering

Holy Mother-Father God,
Divine Loving Light and Heart of the Universe,

I humbly ask for the healing power of your grace to remove my fears about the fate of this world. Keep me from succumbing to the bad news I hear on television and in the newspapers, and falling prey to the endless fearmongering coming from every corner. Help me spread good news and optimism as an antidote to all the darkness being cast across the airwaves. Keep my spirits up and my confidence in the goodness of people strong, and let me forgive and send love to those who have fallen victim to their egos and cause pain in this world. Let me stand for peace and demonstrate my stance by being peaceful myself.

I humbly pray for you to heal this darkness we are in and strengthen the light in the world, beginning with the light in me. Please send in your angels to help all the saddened spirits, and your joy guides to remind us of our true nature and the wonder of being alive. I thank you in advance, with my whole heart and soul, for answering my prayer, and I am ready to serve the light in every way.

Amen and with infinite gratitude.

———— ◆ ————

Freedom from Jealousy

Holy Mother-Father God,
Divine Loving Light and Heart of the Universe,

I humbly ask for the healing power of your grace to free me of the jealousy and insecurity I am struggling with right now. Please send in your angels to help remove this craziness from my heart and fill me with self-love and self-appreciation so that I no longer look to others to validate me. Forgive me for not seeing myself as valuable and for leaving this up to others to determine. I thank you in advance, with my whole heart and soul, for relieving me of this soul-damaging energy and wrapping me up in your love.

Amen and with infinite gratitude.

———— ◆ ————

Retrieving Joy

Holy Mother-Father God,
Divine Loving Light and Heart of the Universe,

I humbly ask for the healing power of your grace to wash away the heaviness in my heart. Grant me the grace to gain fresh perspectives and open myself up to possibilities through positive encounters and new teachers, healers, mentors, and guides. Please send in the joy guides to bring me back to life! I thank you in advance, with my whole heart and soul, for answering my prayer, and I look forward to enjoying a lightness of heart once again.

Amen and with infinite gratitude.

Unfair Judgments

Holy Mother-Father God,
Divine Loving Light and Heart of the Universe,

I humbly ask for the healing power of your grace to help me let go of all the negative assumptions I carry about others. Grant me the clarity to stop these projections, which leave me feeling isolated and cause me to unfairly misread situations and assign blame to individuals. Please send in your angels to free me of these mental and emotional distortions that keep me from letting love in, and help me see others in an accurate and loving light. I thank you in advance, with my whole heart and soul, for answering my prayer and clearing this dreary haze from my view.

Amen and with infinite gratitude.

Competing with or Feeling Threatened by Others

Holy Mother-Father God,
Divine Loving Light and Heart of the Universe,

I humbly ask for the healing power of your grace to help me celebrate others, rather than feel threatened by or competitive with them. Please send in your angels so that I may trust there is enough for everyone, instead of fearing that I will lose out or am less of a person if another succeeds. Let me be a "giver" instead of a "taker" and be inspired by those who succeed around me at all times. I thank you in advance, with my whole heart and soul, for blessing me as you have, and I look forward to sharing these blessings from now on.

Amen and with infinite gratitude.

Blue Skies

Prayers

FOR

Helping Yourself

In this section, you will find prayers to help you get out of your own way by clearing patterns and recognizing blind spots and bad habits that hold you back or interfere with living the life you yearn to have. The aim of these prayers is to evoke good humor, help with your communication, enhance self-care, foster gratitude for your good health, and more.

Blind Spots
and Bad Habits

Holy Mother-Father God,
Divine Loving Light and Heart of the Universe,

I humbly ask for your most blessed grace to fill me with clarity and strength as I confront my shadows and blind spots. Please grant me the ability to be receptive and open to the feedback I receive from others about their frustrations with me, and grant me the willingness to look at myself with their eyes. I pray, quiet my ego's defenses and outrage, and open my heart to learn all that I can. Please awaken in me the wisdom, desire, maturity, and tenacity to consciously address and change my negative behaviors in order to free myself and others of the misery these behaviors bring. Send in your angels to allow me to step out from these shadows and into the light of my true and loving nature. I thank you in advance, with my whole heart and soul, for helping me to grow.

Amen and with infinite gratitude.

Clearing Distraction

Holy Mother-Father God,
Loving Light and Heart of the Universe,

I humbly ask for your most blessed grace to lead me to the place in my heart where I can find you. Grant me the ability to rest my soul and restore my spirit in your ever-loving grace. I pray for you to send in your angels to help silence my mental chatter, which is driving me crazy at the moment, so that I can hear and receive your most benevolent and loving guidance in every cell of my being. By the power and light of your love, I ask for your blessing to clear away all that is not me and does not support my spirit at this time. I thank you in advance, with my whole heart and soul, for quieting my mind and opening my heart to your peace.

Amen and with infinite gratitude.

Relaxing

Holy Mother-Father God,
Divine Loving Light and Heart of the Universe,

I humbly ask for the healing power of your grace to help me move through this day free of the fear that I might miss out on something. Please send in your angels to calm down the urgency that causes me to hurry up, interrupt, and rush those around me. Please help me relax and be present—rather than keep pushing ahead—and trust that all I desire will come to me, in divine time, without my need to chase after it. I thank you in advance, with my whole heart and soul, for answering my prayer and calming my nervous system.

Amen and with infinite gratitude.

Restoration of Good Health

Holy Mother-Father God,
Divine Loving Light and Heart of the Universe,

I humbly ask for the healing power of your grace to restore me to good health. Please send in the spirit healers to guide the doctors and caregivers who are helping me at this time so that their healing efforts—and your unconditional love—flow through them to me and return me to wholeness. I thank you in advance, with my whole heart and soul, for this healing in my life.

Amen and with infinite gratitude.

Forgiving Others

Holy Mother-Father God,
Divine Loving Light and Heart of the Universe,

I humbly ask for the healing power of your grace to help me forgive those who have hurt me. It is so tempting to remain stuck in anger and resentment and feel sorry for myself, and yet I know in my heart that this isn't at all what I want. I accept responsibility for the ways in which I have contributed to what has caused me pain and even see how these experiences have allowed me to learn and grow. Now I pray for you to grant me the power to forgive everyone, including myself. I thank you in advance, with my whole heart and soul, for answering my prayer and helping me move on in peace.

Amen and with infinite gratitude.

Communicating Openly

Holy Mother-Father God,
Divine Loving Light and Heart of the Universe,

I humbly ask for the healing power of your grace to help me communicate honestly and openly with people in my life. Please inspire my words so they express truth and respect for all. I pray, send in your angels to enable me to remain calm and centered and true to myself, even if what I say is not well received at the time or is rejected outright. I especially ask for help to stop my withholding silence, leaving others to second-guess me; instead, let me freely share with others so that our connection has a genuine opportunity to succeed and grow in positive ways. I thank you in advance, with my whole heart and soul, for answering my prayer and easing my way.

Amen and with infinite gratitude.

Stop Neglecting My Health

Holy Mother-Father God,
Divine Loving Light and Heart of the Universe,

I humbly ask for the blessing of your grace so that I stop neglecting my health and begin to treasure and care for myself. Please send in your angels to help me nourish and support my body and give it what it needs so I have the physical and emotional strength to show up in the world with vitality and the confidence to do my best and be my best for others. I thank you in advance, with my whole heart and soul, for answering my prayer, as I am now ready to be responsible for myself in this way.

Amen and with infinite gratitude.

Counting My Blessings
over Fear of Lack

Holy Mother-Father God,
Divine Loving Light and Heart of the Universe,

I humbly ask for the healing power of your grace to take my attention off my concerns over lack of money and help me notice all that is bountiful and working in my life instead. Please help free me of the habit of focusing on what I feel is not enough, while minimizing or ignoring all the abundance you place at my feet. Please send in the angels to help me fully appreciate my life as it is and allow me to feel enriched by it all. I thank you in advance, with my whole heart and soul, for answering my prayer.

Amen and with infinite gratitude.

Supporting Others

Holy Mother-Father God,
Divine Loving Light and Heart of the Universe,

I humbly ask for the healing power of your grace to help me willingly serve the greater good over my own self-interest. Please send in your angels to enable me to champion others' dreams and success as I would my own, knowing that the more I give, the more I receive. Keep me from being selfish or self-absorbed, and help me take a genuine interest in other people's well-being as a way to improve all my relationships, both in my personal life and at work. I thank you in advance, with my whole heart and soul, for answering my prayer, and I am eager to experience the peace this will bring.

Amen and with infinite gratitude.

Healing a Strained Relationship

Holy Mother-Father God,
Divine Loving Light and Heart of the Universe,

I humbly ask for your most blessed grace and guidance during this time of uncertainty in my marriage (or other relationship). Please be my compass in the confusing days ahead and protect me from fear as I work to reestablish a positive, mutually satisfying, and healthy connection between us. I pray for your help to ease our differences and the pain they cause us, and to remember the wonderful things we share that brought us together in the first place. I ask for the humility of spirit to make this my priority over being "right," which is now distancing us. Please send in your angels to banish all the thoughts that leave me feeling threatened or insecure in our connection, and pave our way to reconnection in the heart as we move forward. I thank you in advance, with my whole heart and soul, for answering my prayer, and I confidently await our healing.

Amen and with infinite gratitude.

Finding Self–Love

Holy Mother-Father God,
Divine Loving Light and Heart of the Universe,

Thank you for watching over me. I feel better knowing that you hold me dear and love me unconditionally. I am learning to feel the same way about myself. I humbly ask you to guide me to open my heart and accept all the love that is coming my way today, trusting that those who offer it do so willingly and with pleasure. Help me overcome my fear of being vulnerable, which keeps love out and makes me feel alone and isolated. Wipe clean my negative self-image and distorted self-perceptions, and allow me to see myself as you created me—filled with grace and loving light. Please send in your angels to remind me throughout the day to take a breath and say something positive and loving to myself as an active practice in self-love. I thank you in advance, with my whole heart and soul, for answering my prayer and filling me with your blessings this day.

Amen and with infinite gratitude.

Taking Time Out

Holy Mother-Father God,
Divine Loving Light and Heart of the Universe,

I humbly ask for the healing power of your grace to help me step away when I need to be alone, before I become agitated or unconsciously push others away with my unpleasant moods or behavior as a means to get the space I need. Grant me the wisdom to tune out the external world when I am overloaded and instead turn inward to meditation and prayer so I can rebalance. Give me the self-awareness and self-love I need in order to quietly rejuvenate for a few minutes without feeling guilty or fearful that my self-care is causing me to neglect someone else who needs me. I thank you in advance, with my whole heart and soul, for answering my prayer and helping me become quiet inside.

Amen and with infinite gratitude.

———— ◆ ————

Compassion for Those I Dislike

Holy Mother-Father God,
Divine Loving Light and Heart of the Universe,

I humbly ask for the blessing of your grace to help me find compassion for, and acceptance of, those whom I dislike. Please send in the angels to allow me to see why I have attracted these people to me so that I learn what I must. Then I can either be free of my dislike or be free of them, whichever is best for my spirit. I thank you in advance, with my whole heart and soul, for answering my prayer so that we can all move on in peace.

Amen and with infinite gratitude.

———— ◆ ————

Transition

Holy Mother-Father God,
Divine Loving Light and Heart of the Universe,

I humbly ask for the healing power of your grace to help me stay true to my spirit and faithful to my dreams, even when I meet with adversity or challenge. Please send in your angels to encourage me not to give up and to reach out quickly and ask for help when I need it instead of believing that I must do everything by myself. I especially pray to stay true to my dreams and trust that things will work out, even when it appears as though they won't. I thank you in advance, with my whole heart and soul, for answering my prayer, and I look forward to the support coming my way.

Amen and with infinite gratitude.

Detachment

Holy Mother-Father God,
Divine Loving Light and Heart of the Universe,

I humbly ask for the healing power of your grace to keep me from taking personally the hurtful behaviors of [insert name of individual(s)]. Please send in your angels to help me see my part in this painful dance of reacting to everything being said and done as if it were intentionally meant to hurt me. Change my interpretation so that I may step out of the dance and remain peaceful. I thank you in advance, with my whole heart and soul, for answering my prayer and relieving my stress and upset.

Amen and with infinite gratitude.

———— ✦ ————

Lightening Up

Holy Mother-Father God,
Divine Loving Light and Heart of the Universe,

I humbly ask for the healing power of your grace to allow me to let go of my troubles and enjoy life for a change. Please send in your angels to help me sing a little, dance a little, laugh a little, and take more delight in life than I usually do. I thank you in advance, with my whole heart and soul, for answering my prayer and returning me to joy.

Amen and with infinite gratitude.

———— ◆ ————

Releasing Grudges

Holy Mother-Father God,
Divine Loving Light and Heart of the Universe,

I humbly ask for the healing power of your grace to help me remove all grudges I hold against others and forgive them instead. Please send in your angels so that I may see the gifts these individuals bring to me, even in the form of our differences. I thank you in advance, with my whole heart and soul, for answering my prayer and relieving me of this self-imposed, heavy burden on my heart.

Amen and with infinite gratitude.

Regaining My Humor

Holy Mother-Father God,
Divine Loving Light and Heart of the Universe,

I humbly ask for the healing power of your grace to restore my sense of humor. I have been way too serious for my own good lately and want to lighten up. Grant me the grace to begin by laughing at myself and all the ridiculous things I do and say. Allow me to reconnect with my joy, and trust that all is well in spite of my fears. Please send in your angels to help me surrender my unnecessary heaviness so that I may relax, have more fun, and enjoy life. I thank you in advance, with my whole heart and soul, for answering my prayer and helping me laugh once again.

Amen and with infinite gratitude.

Following the Signs

Prayers

FOR

Guidance

In this section, you will find prayers focused on tuning in to and trusting your intuition, especially as you make decisions and implement changes that will not necessarily make logical sense or be supported by other people in your life. These prayers also ask for assistance in recognizing the subtle support being offered from your higher self, angels, and spiritual guides, who are always there to assist you. Use these prayers to help light your way when you might otherwise be confused.

Listening to
My Inner Voice

Holy Mother-Father God,
Divine Loving Light and Heart of the Universe,

I humbly ask for the healing power of your grace to help me listen to my inner voice instead of remaining stuck in my head and tuning my intuition out. Grant me the courage to stop running from it or denying its presence in my heart, or from having the need for guarantees before I listen or act on my inner guidance. Bless me with the wisdom to trust my guidance as it comes and follow up with action in a timely manner, as I know it is leading me to my highest path of good. I thank you in advance, with my whole heart and soul, for answering my prayer and guiding me as you so lovingly do.

Amen and with infinite gratitude.

Sharpening My Intuition

Holy Mother-Father God,
Divine Loving Light and Heart of the Universe,

I humbly ask for the healing power of your grace to improve my discernment so that I may choose the people I spend time with more wisely. Please send in your angels to help me listen to my intuition when it warns me about someone or something, and have me quickly break away when warned to. Grant me the grace to trust my intuition instead of arguing with it, especially when my ego does not like what it has to say. I thank you in advance, with my whole heart and soul, for answering my prayer and getting me out of my own way.

Amen and with infinite gratitude.

———— ◆ ————

Uncertainty

Holy Mother-Father God,
Divine Loving Light and Heart of the Universe,

I humbly ask for the healing power of your grace to help me sit with uncertainty, rather than try to force answers before their time. Please grant me the faith that all will be made clear in due time, and let me surrender my concerns over to you until then. Please send in your angels to help me calm my anxiety and trust that I will be guided so I can relax. I thank you in advance, with my whole heart and soul, for answering my prayer as I surrender my uncertainty to you.

Amen and with infinite gratitude.

Help from My Higher Self

Holy Mother-Father God,
Divine Loving Light and Heart of the Universe,

I humbly ask for the healing power of your grace to help me shift my focus and behavior away from my lower self and toward my higher self. Please send in your angels to help me do my best and be my best with everyone and in every situation. Remove my self-serving, negative behaviors and suspicious out-look, and replace them with lucid, loving awareness, choices, and actions, which are good for all concerned. I thank you in advance, with my whole heart and soul, for your help, as I am truly ready for a change.

Amen and with infinite gratitude.

Stepping into the Unknown

Holy Mother-Father God,
Divine Loving Light and Heart of the Universe,

I humbly ask for the healing power of your grace to help me step into the unknown, even though I do not feel comfortable doing so. Grant me the grace to engage in new experiences with enthusiasm and a willingness to learn. Please send in your angels to enable me to replace my resistance to change with a sense of adventure and discovery. I thank you in advance, with my whole heart and soul, for answering my prayer and giving me confidence to carry on in faith.

Amen and with infinite gratitude.

Overimpulsiveness

Holy Mother-Father God,
Divine Loving Light and Heart of the Universe,

I humbly ask for the blessing of your grace to help me rein in my impulsive behavior and carefully consider all my options in a grounded, objective way before I do or say anything. Please send in your angels so that I may be conscientious and mindful of the impact my behavior has not only on me but on others as well. I thank you in advance, with my whole heart and soul, for answering my prayer. I will relax now.

Amen and with infinite gratitude.

———— ✦ ————

Extra Support

Holy Mother-Father God,
Divine Loving Light and Heart of the Universe,

I humbly ask for your most blessed generosity in sending any extra angels my way today, as I feel as though what I am facing right now is bigger than my ability to handle. I pray also for the help of all my divine protectors, for with them by my side, I know that I'll be able to more gracefully face what lies before me. Without the extra support, I'm not so sure that I can do this. I thank you in advance, with my whole heart and soul, for answering my prayer and being so generous with me.

Amen and with infinite gratitude.

———— ◆ ————

Making Choices

Holy Mother-Father God,
Divine Loving Light and Heart of the Universe,

I am listening. I humbly ask for you to guide me this day. I am at a fork in the road (at work, in my relationship, over a move, and so forth), and I am not sure which way to go. Release me from my endless ruminations over trying to figure out my next step, as they are exhausting me to no end. I give up. I pray for your help to step back for now and wait for you to show me the way. I thank you in advance, with my whole heart and soul, for hearing my prayer, and I confidently await my direction.

Amen and with infinite gratitude.

Taking Charge of My Life

Holy Mother-Father God,
Divine Loving Light and Heart of the Universe,

I humbly ask for the healing power of your grace to stop me from seeking out others' opinions when I know in my heart what is right for me. Please release my resistance to taking charge of my life and grant me the power to follow my inner guidance easily and without hesitation. Please send in your angels to help me assume full responsibility for my life and trust my intuition as it shows me the way. This is my prayer for today.

Amen and with infinite gratitude.

———— ◆ ————

Calling My Higher Self to Make Decisions

Holy Mother-Father God,
Divine Loving Light and Heart of the Universe,

I humbly ask for the healing power of your grace to help me turn all my decisions over to my higher self from now on. I invoke and empower my higher self to intercept and override any decision I make out of fear, selfishness, or lack of love for myself and others. I pray, send in the angels to clear the way in support of my highest good and keep my mind fully cooperative with my spirit over that of my lower ego nature. I thank you in advance, with my whole heart and soul, for answering my prayer, and I await your blessings in full confidence.

Amen and with infinite gratitude.

——— ◆ ———

Trusting Guidance

Holy Mother-Father God,
Divine Loving Light and Heart of the Universe,

I humbly ask for the healing power of your grace to help me turn all my goals and intentions over to you. Grant me the ability to quiet my mind and tune in to my heart so that I may receive your guidance and trust the outcome. Please send in your angels to allow me to release my limiting ideas and open up to your unlimited ones. I thank you in advance, with my whole heart and soul, for answering my prayer and guiding me to a brighter path.

Amen and with infinite gratitude.

———— ◆ ————

Surrendering
to Divine Will

Holy Mother-Father God,
Divine Loving Light and Heart of the Universe,

I humbly ask for the blessing of your grace to help me follow your will over my own. I am tired of following my ego, as it only leads me to isolation and doesn't bring me any joy. So today, I ask that you move my heart and mind in the direction that you want for me. Make me aware of what I am not noticing, and shift my priorities to those that best support my soul plan and purpose instead of my limited, ego-based agendas. Let me give up insisting that things go my way and learn to listen and go with the divine flow instead. I have reached a dead end and have no idea what to do next. Please show me. This is my prayer for today.

Amen and with infinite gratitude.

Clarity on My Path

Holy Mother-Father God,
Divine Loving Light and Heart of the Universe,

I humbly ask for the healing power of your grace to clear my mind and allow me to get back in tune with my heart. I have no idea what I want or need. Please help me discover my path and lead me there. I thank you in advance, with my whole heart and soul, for shining a light and guiding me when I am so confused.

Amen and with infinite gratitude.

———— ◆ ————

Trusting My Intuition

Holy Mother-Father God,
Divine Loving Light and Heart of the Universe,

I humbly ask for the healing power of your grace to help me listen to my intuition and follow it without question. Let me recognize its subtle signs and no longer pretend I did not notice these vital soul-guiding signals along the way. Allow me to act decisively on the guidance I receive, in a timely manner, and not wait for guarantees before I take steps in the direction in which I am guided to walk. Please send in your angels to turn up the volume so that I will no longer miss my inner guidance, especially in the areas where I need it most right now. I thank you in advance, with my whole heart and soul, for being my guiding light.

Amen and with infinite gratitude.

Lightening the Load

Prayers
TO
Ease
My Way

In this section, you will find prayers asking for help relieving yourself of unnecessary burdens and struggles so that you can seek lightness of heart and soul. These prayers offer guidance for releasing blocks and old patterns, finding freedom from blame and self-pity, letting go of rigidness and obsessions, and more.

Releasing Blocks

Holy Mother-Father God,
Divine Loving Light and Heart of the Universe,

I humbly ask for the healing power of your grace to release all my attachments to people and circumstances that hold me back, make me doubt myself, or cause me to feel insecure and afraid. Please send in your angels to help me attract uplifting people and circumstances from now on. I thank you in advance, with my whole heart and soul, for answering my prayer and clearing the way to brighter, more fulfilling experiences.

Amen and with infinite gratitude.

———— ◆ ————

Freedom from Judgment

Holy Mother-Father God,
Divine Loving Light and Heart of the Universe,

I humbly ask for the healing power of your grace to help me accept others, rather than judge them. Grant me the grace and wisdom to understand that there is no empirical "right" or "wrong" when it comes to people or life—only what feels personally correct for each individual. Help me respect and adhere to my values and morals and ways of doing things without attacking those of other people in my life. If our values, priorities, and ways of doing things are too far apart, let me accept that without casting blame, attacking, or disparaging anyone and go my own way in peace. Wipe all judgment from my heart and replace it with the desire and ability to understand, respect, appreciate, and learn from others, even when we do not agree with one another. This is my heartfelt prayer for today.

Amen and with infinite gratitude.

Releasing Old Patterns

Holy Mother-Father God,
Divine Loving Light and Heart of the Universe,

I humbly ask for the healing power of your grace to alert me when I fall into old patterns that no longer serve me. Please send in your angels to make me so uncomfortable that these patterns do not escape my awareness, and I interrupt myself and quickly realign my actions with my spirit. I thank you in advance, with my whole heart and soul, for answering my prayer, as I am ready to grow in every way now.

Amen and with infinite gratitude.

Following Through

Holy Mother-Father God,
Divine Loving Light and Heart of the Universe,

I humbly ask for your blessing and grace to help me follow through on my commitments to my true goals, instead of dropping them to the wayside or allowing myself to be distracted by other things. Give me confidence that my goals are possible to accomplish, and then enable me to take the daily steps necessary to ensure my success. Please send in the angels so that I may create my heart's desire now instead of deferring my dreams to meet my obligations. Thank you for hearing my prayer and helping me make the changes I want to make.

Amen and with infinite gratitude.

Obsession

Holy Mother-Father God,
Divine Loving Light and Heart of the Universe,

I am struggling with my behavior of obsessing over my relationship (or a specific person or situation) and find myself feeling anxious and insecure because of it. I know this is a lesson for me in finding more love for myself instead of hoping it will come by way of this person (or situation), but today I am not managing this very well. Please keep me from believing that this person's behavior (or this situation, or the lack of my desired outcome) is a reflection of my worth, and help me to not feel insecure, rejected, or angry as a result. Help me maintain unconditional love for both myself and [insert name of individual(s)] so I can release myself from this obsession. This has been so difficult to do on my own. I am ready. Thank you with my whole heart and spirit.

Amen and with infinite gratitude.

Releasing
My Burdens

Holy Mother-Father God,
Divine Loving Light and Heart of the Universe,

I humbly ask for the healing power of your grace to release *all* my burdens today, even the ones I still want to hold on to. Help me let go of my attachment to pain and suffering, and surrender my worries and concerns into your care. Let me trust that my bills will be paid, my home is secure, my family is safe, and that I will be able to meet the responsibilities in my life so there is no need to worry. I pray, send in the angels to reassure me in these difficult moments and allow me to recognize and receive your love and support. I am ready to lighten up and let go. Thank you for helping me do so.

Amen and with infinite gratitude.

Freedom from Blame

Holy Mother-Father God,
Divine Loving Light and Heart of the Universe,

I humbly ask for the healing power of your grace to help me express my feelings in a way that does not blame or attack others and instead communicate in a respectful and productive way. Please open my heart toward the people who frustrate and anger me so that I can learn what I need to learn from them and set the discord aside. Please send in the angels to help me listen to others in the same loving way in which I want to be heard. I thank you in advance, with my whole heart and soul, for answering my prayer and relieving me of this painful and damaging habit.

Amen and with infinite gratitude.

Accepting Myself as I Am

Holy Mother-Father God,
Divine Loving Light and Heart of the Universe,

I humbly ask for the healing power of your grace so that I may accept my shortcomings and replace my self-criticism with self-acceptance and unconditional love. Please send in your angels to free my grip on what darkens my light and causes me to feel so unworthy, and banish it forever. Help me, especially, to be happy and peaceful in my own skin, as God created me. Please free me of the need for other people's approval and have me approve of and love myself instead. Grant me the grace to elevate and preserve my self-esteem, even in the face of those who try to take it away. I thank you in advance, with my whole heart and soul, for answering my prayer and loving me unconditionally.

Amen and with infinite gratitude.

Ending Unhealthy Relationships

Holy Mother-Father God,
Divine Loving Light and Heart of the Universe,

I humbly ask for the healing power of your grace to help me end my relationships with people who are unhealthy and toxic, cause me chronic aggravation and disappointment, and leave me feeling unhappy and drained. Give me the wisdom to know which relationships are worth remaining in and which ones I need to move away from. I humbly ask that you do this in a loving way, even when I am afraid to let go. Please send in the angels to help me quickly move on in peace. I thank all those I now release and bless their way as our shared time comes to an end. I am ready for this prayer to be answered, even if it brings about great change.

Amen and with infinite gratitude.

Easing Rigidity

Holy Mother-Father God,
Divine Loving Light and Heart of the Universe,

I humbly ask for the healing power of your grace to ease my rigid thinking and replace it with open-mindedness so that I no longer back myself into a corner of self-righteousness and make myself miserable. Please send in your angels to help free me of the belief that I must always be "right" and open me up to what I don't know. I thank you in advance, with my whole heart and soul, for answering my prayer and giving me the ease I need in order to grow.

Amen and with infinite gratitude.

Resolving Differences

Holy Mother-Father God,
Divine Loving Light and Heart of the Universe,

I humbly ask for the healing power of your grace to help me find peace with those people in my life with whom I can't seem to get along. I pray that we can let go of our differences and find understanding and acceptance in place of the strife and animosity we now have between us. Please send in your angels to help pave a bridge of mutual respect so that we may meet in the middle and come to a place of peaceful cooperation. I thank you in advance, with my whole heart and soul, for this healing.

Amen and with infinite gratitude.

Surrendering and Trusting in a Positive Outcome

Holy Mother-Father God,
Divine Loving Light and Heart of the Universe,

I humbly ask for the healing power of your grace to help me override my fear and have faith that everything will be okay with me (or my family or friends). Please send in your angels to keep my mind, my heart, and my body at ease, moving in the direction of your divine plan for me. I also pray for the same for my beautiful family, friends, and all people in my life. I thank you in advance, with my whole heart and soul, for answering my prayer, and I place my trust in your care.

Amen and with infinite gratitude.

Nonattachment

Holy Mother-Father God,
Divine Loving Light and Heart of the Universe,

I humbly ask for the healing power of your grace to remove all attachment I have to keeping myself in pain. Grant me the grace to forgive the painful actions of others and to forgive myself for allowing abuse into my life. Please send in your angels to bring me a sign today that you are here, watching over me, so that my soul can start to heal. I thank you in advance, with my whole heart and soul, for answering my prayer, and I confidently await these blessings this day.

Amen and with infinite gratitude.

———— ◆ ————

Difficult Endings

Holy Mother-Father God,
Divine Loving Light and Heart of the Universe,

I humbly ask for the healing power of your grace to help me accept this difficult ending (of a relationship or a job) with strength and keep moving forward with the confidence to create new beginnings. I pray, keep this ending from causing me to doubt myself or feel rejected or inadequate in any way. Allow me to move on in peace, confident in the knowledge that our shared journey has come to its natural completion, and help me release myself from this connection, with blessings and well wishes over resentments and hurt. I am not there yet, but I pray that with your grace, I will soon get there. I am thankful for all the gifts of the past and look forward to the blessings of the next phase in my life.

Amen and with infinite gratitude.

Stop Complaining

Holy Mother-Father God,
Divine Loving Light and Heart of the Universe,

I humbly ask for the healing power of your grace to help me be a pleasant, uplifting person today, rather than complaining or being a "downer." Put a smile on my face and release me from the frown I so often fall into. Help me see the beautiful in life and say so, instead of pointing out the shadows and flaws. Let me provide positive feedback and acknowledgment instead of raining on someone's parade, including my own. I thank you in advance, with my whole heart and soul, for answering my prayer and for your endless love and support as I grow.

Amen and with infinite gratitude.

———— ◆ ————

Freedom from Overthinking

Holy Mother-Father God,
Divine Loving Light and Heart of the Universe,

I humbly ask for the healing power of your grace to free me from overthinking and help me trust my inner guidance instead. Please send in your angels to release me from obsessing over whether something is "right" or "wrong," and let me get on with living a true and authentic life today. I thank you in advance, with my whole heart and soul, for answering my prayer, and I confidently await my inner peace.

Amen and with infinite gratitude.

Dissolving Self–Pity

Holy Mother-Father God,
Divine Loving Light and Heart of the Universe,

I humbly ask for the healing power of your grace to keep me from feeling sorry for myself. Please send in your angels to teach me a new song of gratitude and appreciation for all the blessings in my life. I thank you in advance, with my whole heart and soul, for answering my prayer and for blessing me in countless ways.

Amen and with infinite gratitude.

———— ◆ ————

Fellow Travelers

Prayers

FOR

*Improving
Relationships*

In this section, you will find prayers asking for help in your relationships with others, as you strive to become a more authentic and loving person. Here you will find prayers of gratitude for friends, prayers for overcoming insecurity in your relationships, prayers when struggling with others, prayers for learning to listen better, and more. Using these prayers will assist you in bringing about peace and harmony in all your relationships.

Gratitude for Friends

Holy Mother-Father God,
Divine Loving Light and Heart of the Universe,

I deeply thank you for your most generous blessing of all: the loving people who make my life so wonderful and leave me feeling so supported. I am deeply grateful for the ways in which they encourage me, love me, and keep me close when I feel afraid and alone. Thank you for enriching my life with their gifts, their contributions, their perspectives, their comfort, and their companionship. I am so grateful for their generous blessings, and I thank you with my whole heart and soul for their presence in my life.

Amen and with infinite gratitude.

——— ◆ ———

Overcoming Insecurity in Relationships

Holy Mother-Father God,
Divine Loving Light and Heart of the Universe,

I humbly ask for the healing power of your grace to help me overcome my insecurity and self-doubt in relationship to others and remember that I am a beautiful being of love and light who deserves to be, and can be, fully loved for who I am. Please send in your angels to help me regain my confidence and trust that I am lovable, even if I doubt it. I thank you in advance, with my whole heart and soul, for answering my prayer and loving me as you do.

Amen and with infinite gratitude.

Helping Others

Holy Mother-Father God,
Divine Loving Light and Heart of the Universe,

I humbly ask for the healing power of your grace to help me bring support and uplifting energy into the lives of those who are suffering. Please send in your angels to enable me to offer love to others as a way to experience it more in my own heart. I thank you in advance, with my whole heart and soul, for answering my prayer and guiding me to be a more giving person today.

Amen and with infinite gratitude.

Struggling
with Others

Holy Mother-Father God,
Divine Loving Light and Heart of the Universe,

I know that my enemies are my teachers, but today I am afraid I am flunking the class. I know that my life is my own creation and that what happens in my life mirrors my own self-esteem and self-love, but today I have broken the mirror and am floundering in the broken pieces. I know that love is the door I must open to move forward, but I cannot find the key. I humbly ask for you to send in your angels to help me, for I have lost my way. I thank you in advance, with my whole heart and soul, for answering my prayer, and I confidently await relief.

Amen and with infinite gratitude.

Listening Better

Holy Mother-Father God,
Divine Loving Light and Heart of the Universe,

I humbly ask for the healing power of your grace to help me genuinely listen to others instead of tuning them out, as I so often do. Grant me the willingness to actually hear and respect others, especially those whom I dislike and don't want to hear. I pray, please send in your angels to help me be more open to others, with a compassionate and available heart, so that I may better understand their needs and respect their points of view. I thank you in advance, with my whole heart and soul, for answering my prayer.

Amen and with infinite gratitude.

———— ◆ ————

Slowing Down

Holy Mother-Father God,
Divine Loving Light and Heart of the Universe,

I humbly ask for the healing power of your grace to allow me to slow down enough to feel my feelings and not bypass them with excessive "busy-ness." Grant me the grace to stop talking long enough to hear my inner guidance. Please send in your angels to help me relax into myself. I thank you in advance, with my whole heart and soul, for answering my prayer, and I surrender to your love.

Amen and with infinite gratitude.

Positive Companionship

Holy Mother-Father God,
Divine Loving Light and Heart of the Universe,

I humbly ask for the healing power of your grace to lead me toward supportive people and away from those who undermine my growth. I pray, please send in your beautiful angels to help me know the difference and have the willingness to follow my inner guidance, even when it is uncomfortable to do so. I open my heart and spirit to those who will challenge me to live as a conscious, authentic, and loving human being, and happily accept their challenge. I thank you in advance, with my whole heart and soul, for answering my prayer, and I look forward to my new companions.

Amen and with infinite gratitude.

— ◆ —

Lighting the Way for Others

Holy Mother-Father God,
Divine Loving Light and Heart of the Universe

I humbly ask to use the healing power of your grace to brighten the lives of others, especially those who are clearly in their own darkness. Please engage my smile, warmth, interest, and compassion so that all those with whom I interact today feel seen, loved, and valued by me. Let this be my purpose. I thank you in advance, with my whole heart and soul, for answering my prayer. I am eager to serve with love!

Amen and with infinite gratitude.

Improving My Relationships

Holy Mother-Father God,
Divine Loving Light and Heart of the Universe,

I humbly ask for the healing power of your grace to help me recognize how I am undermining my relationships with others with my moods, my withholding, my acting out, and my ego defenses that make me "right" and others "wrong." I pray, allow me to break free of these patterns once and for all and open my heart with love and acceptance for myself and others. Please send in your angels to raise my personal vibration to a higher, more expanded, and loving frequency so that I can create and sustain the kind of satisfying relationships that I yearn for. I thank you in advance, with my whole heart and soul, for answering my prayer and helping me grow.

Amen and with infinite gratitude.

Being Stubborn

Holy Mother-Father God,
Divine Loving Light and Heart of the Universe,

Please send in your angels to help me stop being so stubborn and self-righteous before I cause more pain to myself or others. Relieve me of my rebelliousness and my fear of being controlled, and allow me to become more receptive and cooperative toward those I share my life with. Help me surrender my self-important perception that my way is always the best way, and open my heart and mind to learning that there are many ways to do things in life. Let me forgive and release my resistance to the influence of others when it is in my best interest to do so, and respect others' needs and way of doing things as much as I do my own. I thank you in advance, with my whole heart and soul, for answering my prayer, as I am sure this will help my relationships with others and bring me greater peace.

Amen and with infinite gratitude.

Being Respectful of Others

Holy Mother-Father God,
Divine Loving Light and Heart of the Universe,

I humbly ask for the blessing of your grace to act with love and respect for myself and others as I move through this day. Please send in your angels to help me slow down and be aware of others, rather than mindlessly run over them on the way to fulfilling my own agenda. Open my vision to see more than what I am looking for so that I may realize how my words and behaviors affect those around me. Allow kindness and appreciation for others to flow through my words, and remind me to say "thank you" often and with sincerity. I thank you for helping me in this way, with my whole heart and soul, and I look forward to these changes in me.

Amen and with infinite gratitude.

Taking Nothing Personally

Holy Mother-Father God,
Divine Loving Light and Heart of the Universe,

I humbly ask for the blessing of your grace to help me take nothing personally. Make me aware of what I can learn from each challenging experience I have, or difficult or disappointing person I encounter, and allow me to use all of these as opportunities to grow my soul. Please keep my fragile ego in check, as it usually misinterprets things as working against me and causes me so much unnecessary pain and suffering. Please send in the angels to help me remember that it's not all about me, and grant me the ability to see beyond my own insecurity. This is my prayer for today.

Amen and with infinite gratitude.

Difficult Relationships

Holy Mother-Father God,
Divine Loving Light and Heart of the Universe,

I humbly ask for the healing power of your grace to keep my heart open as I find my way in the difficult relationship I now have with my partner (or other). Please send in your angels to help me see my part in our struggle and the soul lessons I must now learn so that I may help free this gridlock we are in. Please guide me each step of the way to a deeper, more loving and forgiving heart so that we may find peace and trust in each other and return to the friendship and love we once had. I thank you in advance, with my whole heart and soul, for answering my prayer, and I confidently await your healing.

Amen and with infinite gratitude.

Trusting Others

Holy Mother-Father God,
Divine Loving Light and Heart of the Universe,

I humbly ask for the healing power of your grace to relieve me of the need to control everything and replace my doubt with trust in you and in others. Allow me to co-create instead of co-opt. Please send in your angels so that I may ask for help, and open my heart to receive it. I thank you in advance, with my whole heart and soul, for answering my prayer and building my trust in others.

Amen and with infinite gratitude.

Accepting Others as They Are

Holy Mother-Father God,
Divine Loving Light and Heart of the Universe,

I humbly ask for the healing power of your grace to keep me from being vain enough to think I can transform someone into who I want him or her to be. Stop me from believing I know better for others than they know for themselves. Do not allow me to think I can bend someone's will to serve my own. Please send in the angels to help me respect and appreciate others as they are. Grant me the grace to replace my arrogance with acceptance and love. I thank you in advance, with my whole heart and soul, for answering my prayer and guiding my way toward acceptance.

Amen and with infinite gratitude.

Gratitude for
Painful Soul Lessons

Holy Mother-Father God,
Divine Loving Light and Heart of the Universe,

Thank you for all the gifts I have received from those who have caused me the most pain. I humbly ask for the grace to release my anger and resentment toward them and pray that I may appreciate the gifts they brought to me and let the pain go, so I am free of this heavy energy lingering in my heart. Bless their path so they may find happiness and inner peace as well. I thank you now, with my whole heart and soul, for bringing me to this place of understanding.

Amen and with infinite gratitude.

Blessing Others

Holy Mother-Father God,
Divine Loving Light and Heart of the Universe,

I pray this day for my friends and family. I humbly ask that their lives be blessed with love and their dreams be supported in all ways. May their worries be relieved, and may their prayers be answered. I thank you in advance, with my whole heart and soul, for answering my prayer and showering blessings on us all.

Amen and with infinite gratitude.

Enjoying
the Journey

Prayers

FOR A

*More
Beautiful Life*

In this section, you will find prayers asking for ways to relax and enjoy life fully. Here you will find prayers for attracting money, being more playful and creative, opening your heart to the goodness of life, meeting new responsibilities with confidence, and more. Using these prayers will bring about a sense of confidence and a renewed ability to enjoy life no matter what is occurring.

Opening My Heart

Holy Mother-Father God,
Divine Loving Light and Heart of the Universe,

I humbly ask for the blessing of your grace to help me lay down my defenses and stop pushing others away. Heal the ancient wounds inside of me that resist letting others in, for fear they might hurt me, and allow me to reopen my presently closed heart so that I may receive the love and true friendship I seek from others. Please send in your angels to help me greet the world from a place of self-love, strength, and confidence, and not from a place of fear, weakness, and suspicion. I thank you in advance, with my whole heart and soul, for removing these obstacles to my heart.

Amen and with infinite gratitude.

———— ◆ ————

Gratitude for the Blessings in My Life

Holy Mother-Father God,
Divine Loving Light and Heart of the Universe,

Thank you for the blessing of my health. Thank you for the blessing of my family and my friends. Thank you for the blessing of my creativity. Thank you for the blessing of myriad opportunities you present to me every day. Thank you for this beautiful planet I live on. Thank you for the freedom to be myself. I humbly thank you, with my whole heart and soul, for your most generous blessings, in all these ways and more.

Amen and with infinite gratitude.

Being a
Beacon of Light

Holy Mother-Father God,
Divine Loving Light and Heart of the Universe,

I humbly ask for the healing power of your grace to enable me to listen without trying to "fix" others and to reassure them of their own ability to overcome any obstacles they face. Please send in your angels to help me bring laughter, perspective, clarity, and direction, as I remind others of their inner light. Let me do the same for myself. I thank you in advance, with my whole heart and soul, for answering my prayer and allowing me to be a beacon of light.

Amen and with infinite gratitude.

Spreading My Wings

Holy Mother-Father God,
Divine Loving Light and Heart of the Universe,

I humbly ask for the healing power of your grace to break free from my dead-end relationship and spread my wings. Release me from my willingness to remain so unhappy, and my false belief that I can change my present partner to be the kind of person I want him or her to be. Allow me to accept that our connection is not working and never will, so I can let go. Please send in your angels to help me attract the kind of partner who is available and open to an authentic connection at this time so that I may experience the kind of relationship I really want and am now ready for. I thank you in advance, with my whole heart and soul, for answering my prayer, and I confidently await these blessings.

Amen and with infinite gratitude.

Attracting Money

Holy Mother-Father God,
Divine Loving Light and Heart of the Universe,

I humbly ask for the healing power of your grace to dissolve my limiting thoughts and self-sabotaging beliefs about money. I pray, redirect my focus to believing in myself and my ability to easily attract money by doing work that I love and putting love into all the work that I do. I pray, please send in your angels to help me reclaim the power I possess to create the financial success that I want, using the gifts and talents I am blessed with. I thank you in advance, with my whole heart and soul, for answering my prayer and easing my fear.

Amen and with infinite gratitude.

———— ◆ ————

Being More Playful

Holy Mother-Father God,
Divine Loving Light and Heart of the Universe,

I humbly ask for the healing power of your grace for the inspiration to do something fun and playful today, instead of the same old boring things I usually do. Free me from my strict, self-imposed routines that do not allow others in and keep me trapped in my own monotonous drudgery. Please send in your angels with invitations from others so that I may go out and get involved in new things, and have me say *yes* every time. I thank you in advance, with my whole heart and soul, for answering my prayer.

Amen and with infinite gratitude.

———— ◆ ————

Feeling the Goodness of Life

Holy Mother-Father God,
Divine Loving Light and Heart of the Universe,

I humbly ask for the healing power of your grace to remove my resistance to happiness and peace. Please send in your angels to help me feel and embody the goodness of life, and use my talents to share it with others. I thank you in advance, with my whole heart and soul, for answering my prayer, and I confidently await these blessings this day.

Amen and with infinite gratitude.

———— ◆ ————

Confidence in the Midst of Change

Holy Mother-Father God,
Divine Loving Light and Heart of the Universe,

I humbly ask for the healing power of your grace to increase my confidence. I feel uncertain and insecure in the midst of so much change and realize I may cause others to feel the same. Please forgive and release everything that blocks or undermines my feelings of self-love and worthiness. Grant me the grace to raise my self-esteem and awaken in me the highest expression of my beautiful spirit. Please send in your angels to help me lovingly shine out in the world and confidently move forward as I find my way. Surround me with your love so that I may always feel grounded and safe through these changing times and can reassure rather than upset those around me. I thank you in advance, with my whole heart and soul, for answering my prayer.

Amen and with infinite gratitude.

Taking Risks

Holy Mother-Father God,
Divine Loving Light and Heart of the Universe,

I humbly ask for the healing power of your grace for the courage to take the risks I have been avoiding. Replace my hesitation and fear with full trust in my spirit. Allow me to step beyond my comfort zone and experience more of this wonderful life and my own spirit than my fears have allowed me to experience. Please send in your angels to help me believe in myself and finally go after my dreams. I am ready.

Amen and with infinite gratitude.

Freedom from Obsession about My Weight

Holy Mother-Father God,
Divine Loving Light and Heart of the Universe,

I humbly ask for the healing power of your grace to relieve me of my unhealthy obsession with my weight and physical appearance. I pray to move past this fear of being unacceptable to others in this body and feel good in my skin as I am. Please send in your angels to redirect my energy toward loving my body as it is, treating it with respect, embracing balanced and healthy eating habits, exercising daily, and not worrying about my weight anymore. Let me think about things that bring love and light to my heart. This is my deepest prayer for today.

Amen and with infinite gratitude.

——— ✦ ———

Being Open to Good Things

Holy Mother-Father God,
Divine Loving Light and Heart of the Universe,

I humbly ask for the healing power of your grace to readily expect good things to come my way today so that I open myself to all the blessings of the Universe and don't close myself off to anything out of fear of being hurt or disappointed. I thank you in advance, with my whole heart and soul, for answering my prayer and opening my heart to the goodness of life once again.

Amen and with infinite gratitude.

———— ◆ ————

Learning Soul Lessons

Holy Mother-Father God,
Divine Loving Light and Heart of the Universe,

I am open to learning all that serves my growth, lifts my spirit, and helps me better serve others and you. I humbly ask for you to send in the angels and spirit helpers to enable me to fulfill this desire. Fill me with your grace, and let it flow through all I say and do. I thank you in advance, with my whole heart and soul, for answering my prayer and allowing me to learn these soul lessons.

Amen and with infinite gratitude.

———— ◆ ————

Creativity and Play

Holy Mother-Father God,
Divine Loving Light and Heart of the Universe,

I humbly ask for the healing power of your grace to unleash my creative spirit. Grant me the grace to sing out, dance with abandon, make crazy music, paint messy pictures, and create as I once did as a child. Please send in your angels to help liberate the part of me that loves to create for the joy of it. I thank you in advance, with my whole heart and soul, for answering my prayer and helping me free myself.

Amen and with infinite gratitude.

Finding Solutions

Holy Mother-Father God,
Divine Loving Light and Heart of the Universe,

I humbly ask for the healing power of your grace to help me leave behind the world of problems and place my focus on creatively finding solutions instead. Please send in your angels to turn my attention toward asking new questions, exploring new avenues, and leaving no stone unturned as I begin to solve my problems, while refraining from creating new ones. Help me get out of my own way and into the life I am intended to enjoy. I thank you in advance, with my whole heart and soul, for answering my prayer.

Amen and with infinite gratitude.

Trusting the Divine Plan

Holy Mother-Father God,
Divine Loving Light and Heart of the Universe,

I humbly ask for the healing power of your grace to help me remember that everything in life happens for a reason; please send in your angels to help me discover that reason. Please keep me from falling under the spell and seduction of victimhood that leads me to take painful events in my life personally and keeps me from being able to respond to what I am confronted with in an empowered and self-loving way. Give me the resilience to face my challenges (even when they seem insurmountable) with strength, courage, and the ability to carry on with creativity and grace. I thank you in advance, with my whole heart and soul, for answering my prayer.

Amen and with infinite gratitude.

Enjoying Life

Holy Mother-Father God,
Divine Loving Light and Heart of the Universe,

I humbly ask for the healing power of your grace to help me enjoy life today and not complain. Please grant me the ability to be optimistic and see the glass as half-full rather than half-empty. Help me ease my overly strict, self-depriving tendencies so that I can have fun. Allow me to give myself permission to take time out to smell the roses, taste the chocolate, and enjoy the sweetness in life, instead of aggressively rushing through the day and missing it all. I thank you in advance, with my whole heart and soul, for answering my prayer and for blessing my life.

Amen and with infinite gratitude.

Seeing the
Light in Everyone

Holy Mother-Father God,
Divine Loving Light and Heart of the Universe,

I humbly ask for the healing power of your grace to help me see the holy light of goodness in myself and in others, and release everything in me that sees anything else. I thank you in advance, with my whole heart and soul, for answering my prayer, and I confidently await these blessings.

Amen and with infinite gratitude.

Meeting New Responsibilities

Holy Mother-Father God,
Divine Loving Light and Heart of the Universe,

I humbly ask for the healing power of your grace to keep my mind open and my focus sharp, as new demands are being asked of me (at home, at work, with family) right now. Please help me rise to the occasion, quickly learn the tasks at hand, do what I must do, and not let down those who count on me. Please send in your angels and spirit helpers to show me how best to succeed and not get overwhelmed, resentful, or insecure. I thank you in advance, with my whole heart and soul, for answering my prayer and helping me find my confidence.

Amen and with infinite gratitude.

Freedom from Frustration

Holy Mother-Father God,
Divine Loving Light and Heart of the Universe,

Thank you for challenging me to let go of control through the help of those who cause me so much frustration. In my interactions with them, I am learning to be more patient, understanding, and accepting of differences, which in the long run will only make my life much easier. I bless and thank their spirits for having taken on this unpleasant role in my life. And I thank you, with my whole heart and soul, for this present opportunity.

Amen and with infinite gratitude.

New Horizons

Prayers

FOR

*More Love
and Light*

In this section, you will find prayers to help open your heart to love, recognizing and receiving all the love the Universe is showering upon you. Here you will find prayers of gratitude, prayers for ways to be of service, prayers that express kindness and compassion for all beings, and more. Using these prayers will help you raise your personal vibration and lead you to a higher, unconditionally loving frequency.

Gratitude for
Help Lifting the Darkness

Holy Mother-Father God,
Divine Loving Light and Heart of the Universe,

Thank you for lighting my way through the darkness and for keeping my heart open to your love and guidance. I feel your presence in my heart and in my bones, clearing and cleansing the old and making way for the new. I am grateful for your love.

Amen and with infinite gratitude.

———— ◆ ————

Gratitude for the Small Things

Holy Mother-Father God,
Divine Loving Light and Heart of the Universe,

Thank you for the small things that make my life so wonderful. Thank you for my good cup of coffee. Thank you for the lovely flowers in my garden. Thank you for the comfortable chair I sit in and the good pillow I sleep on. Thank you for my sweet animal(s) and the trees outside my door. Thank you for the beautiful music I am listening to on the radio (or iPod.) Thank you for all this sweetness and more. I thank you, with my whole heart and soul, for these simple blessings in my life.

Amen and with infinite gratitude.

——— ◆ ———

Learning Lessons

Holy Mother-Father God,
Divine Loving Light and Heart of the Universe,

I humbly ask for the healing power of your grace to understand the value of all the difficult experiences in my life so far and recognize the gifts they have each brought to me. Please send in your angels so that I may now freely move on, no longer attached to the pain, while accepting the gifts. I thank you in advance, with my whole heart and soul, for answering my prayer, and I confidently await these blessings this day.

Amen and with infinite gratitude.

Compassion

Holy Mother-Father God,
Divine Loving Light and Heart of the Universe,

I humbly ask for the healing power of your grace to help me find acceptance of and compassion for all. I am not fully there yet, but I am getting closer. Please send in the angels to help me keep my heart open so that it becomes the only way in which I interact with people in life. I thank you in advance, with my whole heart and soul, for answering my prayer and steadily growing my compassion and loving-kindness.

Amen and with infinite gratitude.

———— ◆ ————

Being Kind
and Loving

Holy Mother-Father God,
Divine Loving Light and Heart of the Universe,

I humbly ask for the healing power of your grace to help me become a more loving person. I pray that my words are kind and loving to all with whom I speak. I pray that my actions are patient and loving to all with whom I interact. I pray that my thoughts are accepting and loving to all on whom I bestow them, including myself. I pray that I am surrounded by love and spread it wherever I go. I thank you in advance, with my whole heart and soul, for answering my prayer, and I confidently await these blessings this day.

Amen and with infinite gratitude.

Freedom from Karma

Holy Mother-Father God,
Divine Loving Light and Heart of the Universe,

I humbly ask for forgiveness and I extend forgiveness to all the people to whom I am in karmic debt from this moment forward. Please send in your angels to help me transmute my pain into understanding and gratitude for the lessons I am learning and the gifts I have received. I thank you in advance, with my whole heart and soul, for answering my prayer.

Amen and with infinite gratitude.

Gratitude for Abundance

Holy Mother-Father God,
Divine Loving Light and Heart of the Universe,

Thank you for helping me attract more abundance to my life so that I am able to relax and pay my bills with ease. Thank you for allowing me to share my gifts and talents in the most productive and creative way, and to receive generous compensation as a result. I thank you, with my whole heart and soul, for answering my prayers and granting me these blessings.

Amen and with infinite gratitude.

Loving Fully

Holy Mother-Father God,
Divine Loving Light and Heart of the Universe,

I humbly ask for the healing power of your grace to keep my heart fully open, even though I know it may be broken if I do. Grant me the grace to love with the entirety of my being, even if my love is not returned. Grant me the courage to love fully, even when my beloveds do not receive my love. Please send in your angels to help me love myself through it all, no matter what. I thank you in advance, with my whole heart and soul, for answering my prayer and offering these blessings.

Amen and with infinite gratitude.

Serving Others

Holy Mother-Father God,
Divine Loving Light and Heart of the Universe,

I commit my spirit to you. Use me this day. Use my mind, use my heart, and use my body in the service of others. I place my free will in your care and ask that you please send in your angels to show me the way to serve your plan over my own. I thank you in advance, with my whole heart and soul, for answering my prayer and allowing me to lovingly be of service.

Amen and with infinite gratitude.

———— ◆ ————

Changing Course

Holy Mother-Father God,
Divine Loving Light and Heart of the Universe,

I pray for inspiration today. I humbly ask for the healing power of your grace to clear my perception and wake up my spirit so that I stop wasting time and energy on what I don't love and get on with doing something I do love. I thank you in advance, with my whole heart and soul, for helping me move in the direction of love, and I confidently await my change of direction.

Amen and with infinite gratitude.

———— ◆ ————

Amen and
So It Is

Holy Mother-Father God,
Divine Loving Light and Heart of the Universe,

I thank you for the grace you have showered upon me for all of my days. I thank you for all the generous blessings of my life. I thank you for your ceaseless love for my soul. I accept your grace, blessings, and love and thank you with all my heart and soul.

Amen and with infinite gratitude.

———— ◆ ————

Respecting the Earth

Holy Mother Earth,
Divine Loving Source of All Life,

Thank you for this gorgeous planet we live on. Thank you for the majestic mountains and the beautiful seas. Thank you for giving us the gifts of the bounty of the fields and the air that we breathe. Thank you for your infinite beauty and for the endless blessings this planet offers us. Please forgive us for how we have so deeply wounded and disrespected you in so many ways. Wake up our spirits and help even the densest of beings on the planet realize that as we harm you, we harm ourselves. Let us learn quickly before we cause harm we cannot reverse. Please hear my prayer.

Amen and with infinite gratitude.

Peace in the World

Holy Mother-Father God,
Divine Loving Light and Heart of the Universe,

I pray for the healing of the world today. I pray for the healing of those in the chaos of war. I pray for those who are injured and have lost their homes. I pray for those who have lost their families. I pray for those who have lost their safety. I pray for those who have lost their lives. I pray for those who have lost contact with their heart and spirit. I ask their hearts to wake up and their humanity to return so that we may all be free of fear. I pray, forgive us all.

Amen and with infinite gratitude.

Coming Home to My Spirit

Prayers
OF
Love
AND
Appreciation

In this section, you will find prayers of gratitude and appreciation, prayers requesting blessings and grace, and prayers helping you celebrate life. These prayers will fill your heart with joy and inner peace, and help you finally feel at home in your beautiful spirit and true self.

Gratitude
for Your Grace

Holy Mother-Father God,
Divine Loving Light and Heart of the Universe,

Your grace fills me up. I feel your loving presence all around. I experience you in my wonderful friends and family. I experience you in work. I experience you in the warmth of my home. I experience you in the abundance of food at my table. I experience you in the talents of those around me. I even experience you in painful moments, as I know your grace is with me as I grow. I am so grateful.

Amen and with infinite gratitude.

———— ◆ ————

Only Love

Holy Mother-Father God,
Divine Loving Light and Heart of the Universe,

I love you. I love you. I love you. I love me. I love
me. I love me.

Amen and with infinite gratitude.

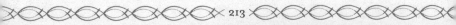

Spreading Joy

Holy Mother-Father God,
Divine Loving Light and Heart of the Universe,

I humbly ask for the healing power of your grace to put a smile on my face and open the curtains to my heart so that I allow your love and light to shine through me. Please send in your angels to help me spread joy to all those I meet. Please let my laughter ripple out wherever I go, summoning the joy guides to join with me, so that I spread positive, uplifting energy everywhere I go. I thank you in advance, with my whole heart and soul, for answering my prayer this day.

Amen and with infinite gratitude.

Bringing the Love

Holy Mother-Father God,
Divine Loving Light and Heart of the Universe,

I humbly ask for the healing power of your grace to make me a source of humor, positivity, and ease in the presence of everyone I meet. Please send in your angels to help me remember that bringing love is the most important work of all. I thank you in advance, with my whole heart and soul, for answering my prayer and allowing me to bring more love into the world.

Amen and with infinite gratitude.

Thanking the Spiritual Guardians

Holy Mother-Father God,
Divine Loving Light and Heart of the Universe,

Thank you, guardians in the spirit world, who watch over me and help me along the way. Thank you for guiding my thoughts and my attention, as well as my feet, so that when I become lost, I return, and when I become afraid, I feel your presence and find my confidence and courage once again. I am so grateful. I humbly thank you with all my heart for your assistance.

Amen and with infinite gratitude.

———— ◆ ————

Gratitude for My Inner Peace

Holy Mother-Father God,
Divine Loving Light and Heart of the Universe,

Thank you for the peace of mind I am experiencing. Thank you for the love and support surrounding me. Thank you for the wisdom to let things in the past go and for my ability to move on in peace. Thank you for healing my wounded heart. I thank you, with my whole heart and soul, for these blessings in my life.

Amen and with infinite gratitude.

Blessing Our Meal

Holy Mother-Father God,
Divine Loving Light and Heart of the Universe,

Thank you for the beautiful meal you set before us and for allowing us to share this wonderful repast with those we love. May it nourish us—body, mind, and soul—and give us the strength of spirit and heart to allow us to continue to share your love and light with all people. We are deeply grateful for your blessing.

Amen and with infinite gratitude.

Hallelujah

Holy Mother-Father God,
Divine Loving Light and Heart of the Universe,

Fill my heart today with song. Lift my voice, and let me sing your praises. I have been given the gift of so many blessings, and I want to let the world know of my love for you. Hallelujah. Hallelujah. Hallelujah.

Amen and with infinite gratitude.

Walking in Grace

Holy Mother-Father God,
Divine Loving Light and Heart of the Universe,

I humbly ask for the healing presence of your grace so that I may greet the world today as you would. I pray for your grace to be the light in my eyes, the smile on my face, and the kind and patient presence in my heart as I connect with others. Please send in your angels to help me offer the love I seek, knowing in this way it will come. I thank you in advance, with my whole heart and soul, for answering my prayer.

Amen and with infinite gratitude.

———— ◆ ————

Appreciation for God's Help

Holy Mother-Father God,
Divine Loving Light and Heart of the Universe,

Thank you for guiding me so beautifully through all the years of my life. Thank you for your steady, calm presence, which I feel in every beat of my heart. Thank you for waking me up when I have fallen asleep. Thank you for the discomfort I have felt when I have lied to myself or to others. Thank you for encouraging me to step beyond my fears and take risks. Thank you for the ability to laugh at myself and enjoy life. Thank you for the great ideas that you have given me and for allowing me to express them. Thank you for the people who love me. Thank you for clearing my confusion. Thank you for your unceasing love as I find my way home.

I thank you, with my whole heart and soul, for granting me so many blessings.

Amen and with infinite gratitude.

A Final Prayer

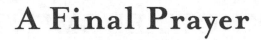

Since completing my pilgrimage on the Camino de Santiago, my life has continued to be challenging. I endured a very painful divorce, put my home up for sale, simplified my whole existence, and moved to Paris to start all over again . . . none of which was easy.

And yet, through all the ups and downs, my heart has remained at peace because I'm constantly reassured by the ever-flowing love, guidance, and support of our Holy Mother-Father God, which I experience when I pray.

I am sure that your life, too, has its share of challenges—that's just the nature of being human. Life is temporary, and change is inevitable. But it is also beautiful and wondrous beyond belief.

And I assure you, with all my heart and soul, that you will experience the wonder and beauty of your life, as I have, if you pray every day.

It's also my greatest prayer that your heart find deep and lasting peace, no matter what unfolds.

All my love,

Sonia

ACKNOWLEDGMENTS

I would like to offer my deepest gratitude and appreciation to those who answered my prayers and helped me bring this prayer book into being. To my wonderful daughters, Sonia and Sabrina, who encouraged me as I wrote, and to my dear friend Mara Zimmerman, who lovingly read each prayer and offered her invaluable feedback, I thank you all with all my heart. I would also like to thank my fantastic editor, Linda Kahn, who helped shape and organize these prayers into the beautiful book that it now is. Thank you once again for your glorious help, Linda. I also am deeply thankful for my great Hay House editors, Lisa Bernier and Lindsay DiGianvittorio, for bringing this prayer book to life with your elegant contributions and genius. And to my angels and guides, who hear my prayers and deliver them to the Holy Mother-Father God on my behalf. I am grateful.

ABOUT THE AUTHOR

Sonia Choquette is celebrated worldwide as an author, spiritual teacher, six-sensory consultant, and a transformational visionary guide. An enchanting storyteller, she is known for her delightful humor and adept skill in quickly shifting people out of psychological and spiritual difficulties, and into a healthier energy flow. Sonia is the author of 19 internationally best-selling books about intuitive awakening, personal and creative growth, and the innate leadership capabilities that reside within, most notably with the *New York Times* bestseller *The Answer Is Simple.*

Sonia's work has been published in over 40 countries and translated into 37 languages, making her one of the most widely read authors and experts in her field of work. Because of her unique gifts, her expertise is sought throughout the world, helping both individuals and organizations dramatically improve their experience and abilities to perform at optimal levels through empowerment and transformation.

Sonia's extensive background in uplifting guidance began as early as 12 years of age; she established her unwavering integrity at this young age, and continued following along this guided path to help other people find their truest selves through intuition. Sonia's legacy is continued by her two daughters, Sonia and Sabrina, who both have their own careers in spiritual coaching and guidance.

Sonia's philanthropic work has brought her to workshops in South Africa, through her publisher Hay House, which helped her set up organizational collaborations with Nurturing Orphans of AIDS for Humanity (NOAH), in addition to extensive charity work and fund-raising throughout the United States.

In 2012 Sonia was awarded the Leader of the Year by the Global Holistic Psychology Association and the award for Exceptional Human Service by the 1st Global Parliament of Human Spirituality in Hyderabad, India.

Sonia attended the University of Denver and the Sorbonne in Paris, and holds a doctorate from the American Institute of Holistic Theology. She is a member of the Transformational Leadership Council and is the host of her own weekly radio show, *Six Sensory Living*.

When not globe-trotting, Sonia can be found in Paris, France. She is an avid traveler and prides herself on her passionate pursuit of learning and growing every day. In her spare time, she enjoys dancing, playing the piano, fashion, art, and design; and she practices yoga and Pilates to stay in shape. To learn more about Sonia, please visit www.soniachoquette.com.

Prayers

Prayers

Prayers

Prayers

Prayers

Prayers